Contents

1. About the Workbook

2. Sticky Solutions

3. The Ps of Anxiety
   - Predictability
   - Permission
   - Perception
   - Perfectionism
   - Pessimism
   - Prevention
   - Present
   - Physical Impact

5. Scarcity: Money, Time, Energy

6. Trauma: Looking Through a New Lens

7. Journal: Your Overcoming Journey

About the Workbook

This workbook is intended to accompany your personal journey to overcome anxiety. It correlates with the book, *Overcoming Anxiety. Sticky Solutions from the Classroom to the Boardroom*. Like most things, you will get out of this workbook directly in proportion to what you invest into the healing work. Consider setting aside a time each day for one month to utilize the workbook and make progress in overcoming anxiety.

Anxiety affects most of us during our lives. This workbook will help you explore and consider some contributors to anxiety. It also aims to help you identify solutions that stick to build new thought patterns and behavioral processes that can help minimize your anxiety, and increase wellness. Three anxiety assessments are placed throughout the workbook to help you consider your progress.

Journaling is an important practice that can help you express, process, and witness your own transformation. The second half of this workbook includes 31 pages of journaling. It can be helpful to journal each day for one month as you work your way through your personal journey to overcoming anxiety. At the end of the month, it can be so rewarding to look back, and review just how far you have come! Let's JUMP!

This workbook will guide you to take a systematic approach to developing a personal plan to overcome anxiety with solutions that stick for you!

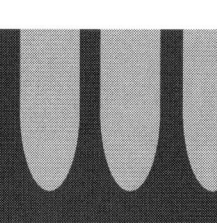

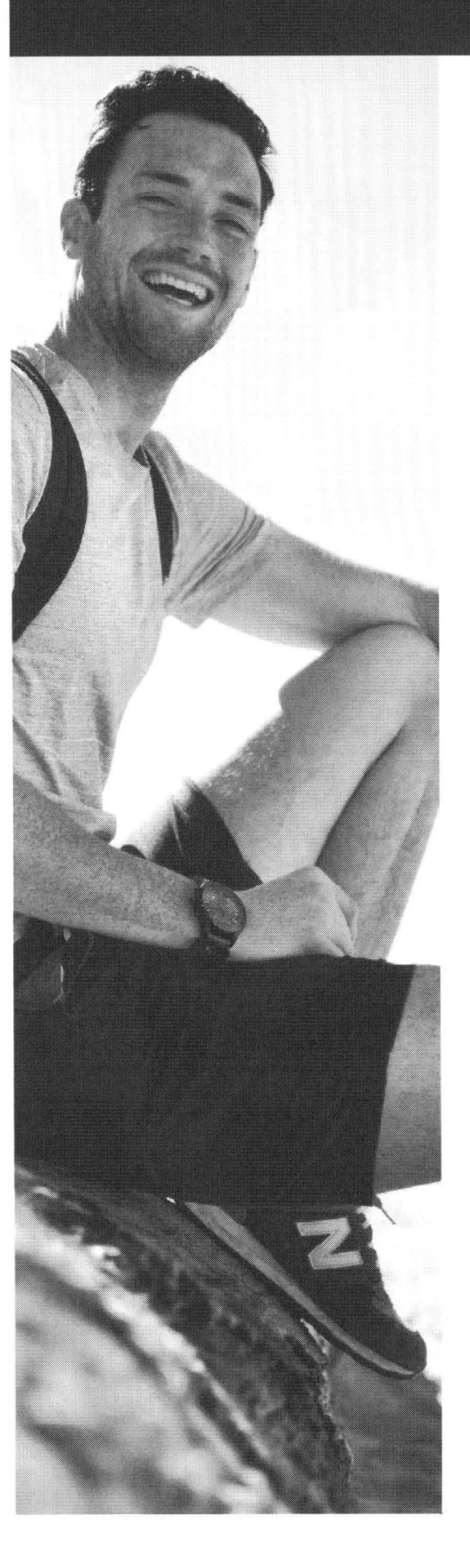

Commitment to Overcoming Anxiety

Identify a time each day that you can commit to the workbook. There are <u>61</u> pages of guided lessons. Try to do 2-3 pages each day, including journaling. Don't be tempted to put it off. You can start NOW!

You may feel challenged, encouraged, grieved, and unsure at times during this work. Accept your feelings as valid and real, and press on!

Don't forget to journal. You may write a few words in list form or elaborate paragraphs, but take a moment each day to reflect on the work you are accomplishing on this healing journey!

OVERCOMING...

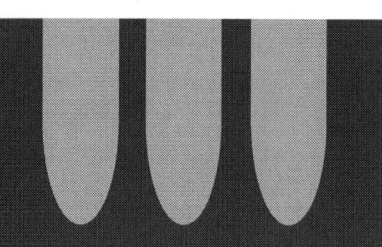

Answer the following questions

✳ What is something you have always wanted to do, but haven't yet accomplished?

✳ What barriers are holding you back?

✳ How would your life change if you could take a GIANT leap and JUMP into this?

01 GAD-7
Generalized Anxiety Disorder Scale

Over the last 2 weeks, how often have you been bothered by the following problems?	Not at all	Several days	Over half the days	Nearly every day
1. Feeling nervous, anxious, or on edge	0	1	2	3
2. Not being able to stop or control worrying	0	1	2	3
3. Worrying too much about different things	0	1	2	3
4. Trouble relaxing	0	1	2	3
5. Being so restless that it is hard to sit still	0	1	2	3
6. Becoming easily annoyed or irritable	0	1	2	3
7. Feeling afraid as if something awful might happen	0	1	2	3
Add the score for each column				
Total Score (add the column scores) =				

Consider the impact of anxiety on your functioning:
How difficult have these made it for you to do your work, take care of things at home, or getting along with other people?

- ☐ Not difficult at all
- ☐ Somewhat difficult
- ☐ Very difficult
- ☐ Extremely difficult

Source: Spitzer RL, Kroenke K, Williams JBW, Lowe B. A brief measure for assessing generalized anxiety disorder. Arch Inern Med. 2006;166:1092-1097.

01 GAD-7

Generalized Anxiety Disorder Scale

Let's get a starting point as you consider your anxiety and your personal journey to overcoming. Record the total score and date of this 1st screening. Please read and consider the disclaimers below.

Scoring GAD-7 Anxiety Severity

Total score for the 7 items ranges from 0 to 21.

- ☐ 0–4: minimal anxiety
- ☐ 5–9: mild anxiety
- ☐ 10–14: moderate anxiety
- ☐ 15–21: severe anxiety

Score: _____   Date: _____

Disclaimer: The Generalized Anxiety Disorder 7-item (GAD-7) scale is a self-administered tool designed to screen for and measure the severity of generalized anxiety disorder. While it can provide valuable insights into your anxiety levels, it is not a substitute for professional medical advice, diagnosis, or treatment.

Informational Purposes Only: The results of the GAD-7 are intended for informational and educational purposes only.

Not a Professional Assessment: This tool does not replace a comprehensive evaluation by a licensed mental health professional. Only a qualified healthcare provider can diagnose anxiety or any other mental health disorder.

Seek Professional Help: If you have concerns about your mental health or if the GAD-7 indicates high levels of anxiety, please seek advice from a healthcare provider. If you are experiencing a mental health crisis, contact emergency services immediately.

Limitations: The GAD-7 has limitations and can not capture all aspects of your mental health.

Source: Spitzer RL, Kroenke K, Williams JBW, Lowe B. A brief measure for assessing generalized anxiety disorder. Arch Inern Med. 2006;166:1092-1097.

Sticky Solutions

As work through and explore, use these pages to record some of the sticky solutions you believe will help you overcome anxiety.

Tip: Don't limit helpful ideas to these pages, consider grabbing a real sticky note pad. Add these solutions to your mirror, bedside table, workstation, car console, kitchen cabinet, or any location that helps remind you that you ARE overcoming!

Sticky Solutions

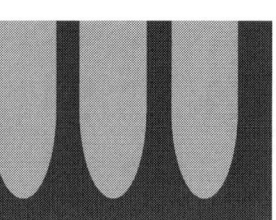

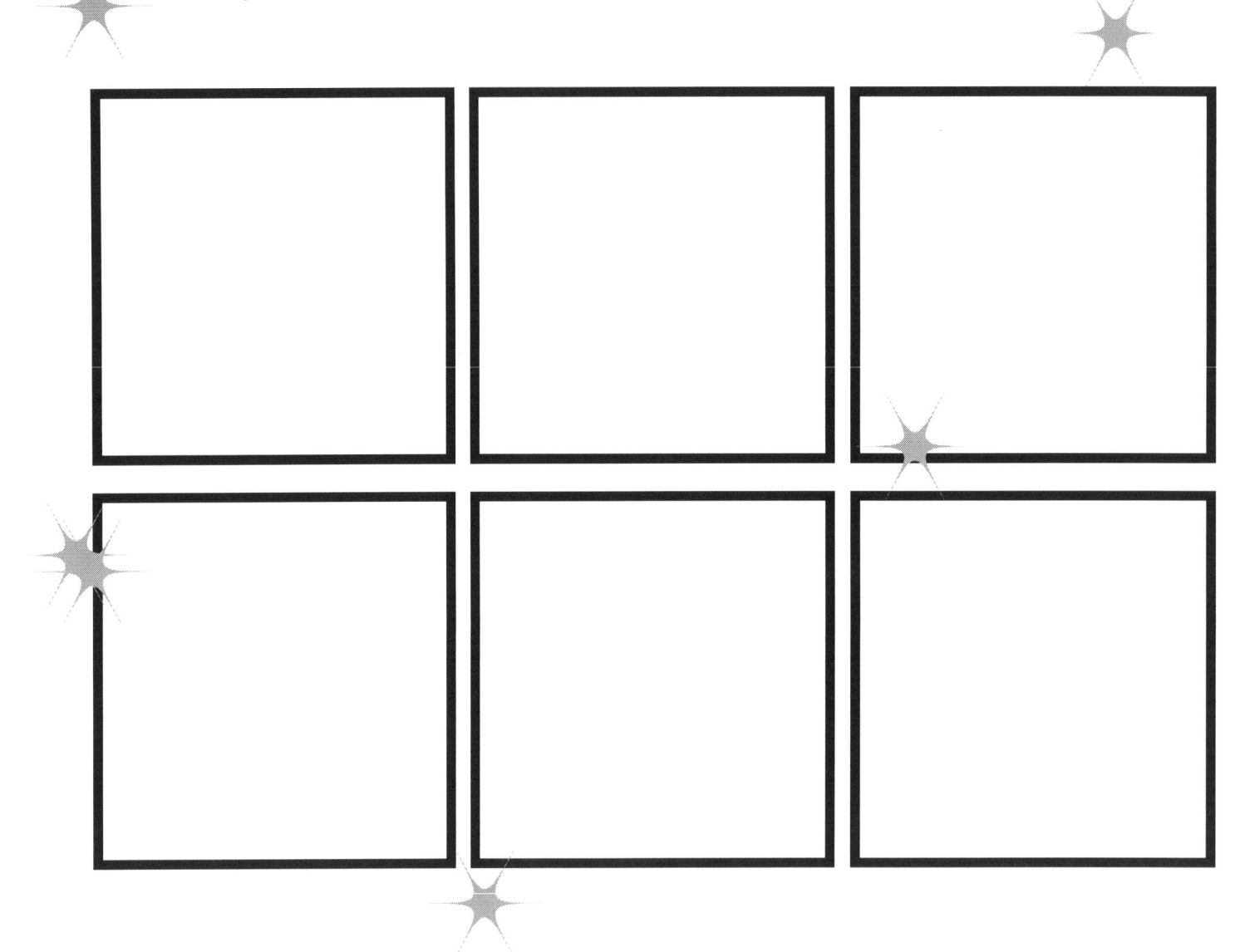

As work through and explore, use these pages to record some of the sticky solutions you believe will help you overcome anxiety.

Tip: Don't limit helpful ideas to these pages, consider grabbing a real sticky note pad. Add these solutions to your mirror, bedside table, workstation, car console, kitchen cabinet, or any location that helps remind you that you ARE overcoming!

Sticky Solutions

As work through and explore, use these pages to record some of the sticky solutions you believe will help you overcome anxiety.

Tip: Don't limit helpful ideas to these pages, consider grabbing a real sticky note pad. Add these solutions to your mirror, bedside table, workstation, car console, kitchen cabinet, or any location that helps remind you that you ARE overcoming!

Sticky Solutions

As work through and explore, use these pages to record some of the sticky solutions you believe will help you overcome anxiety.

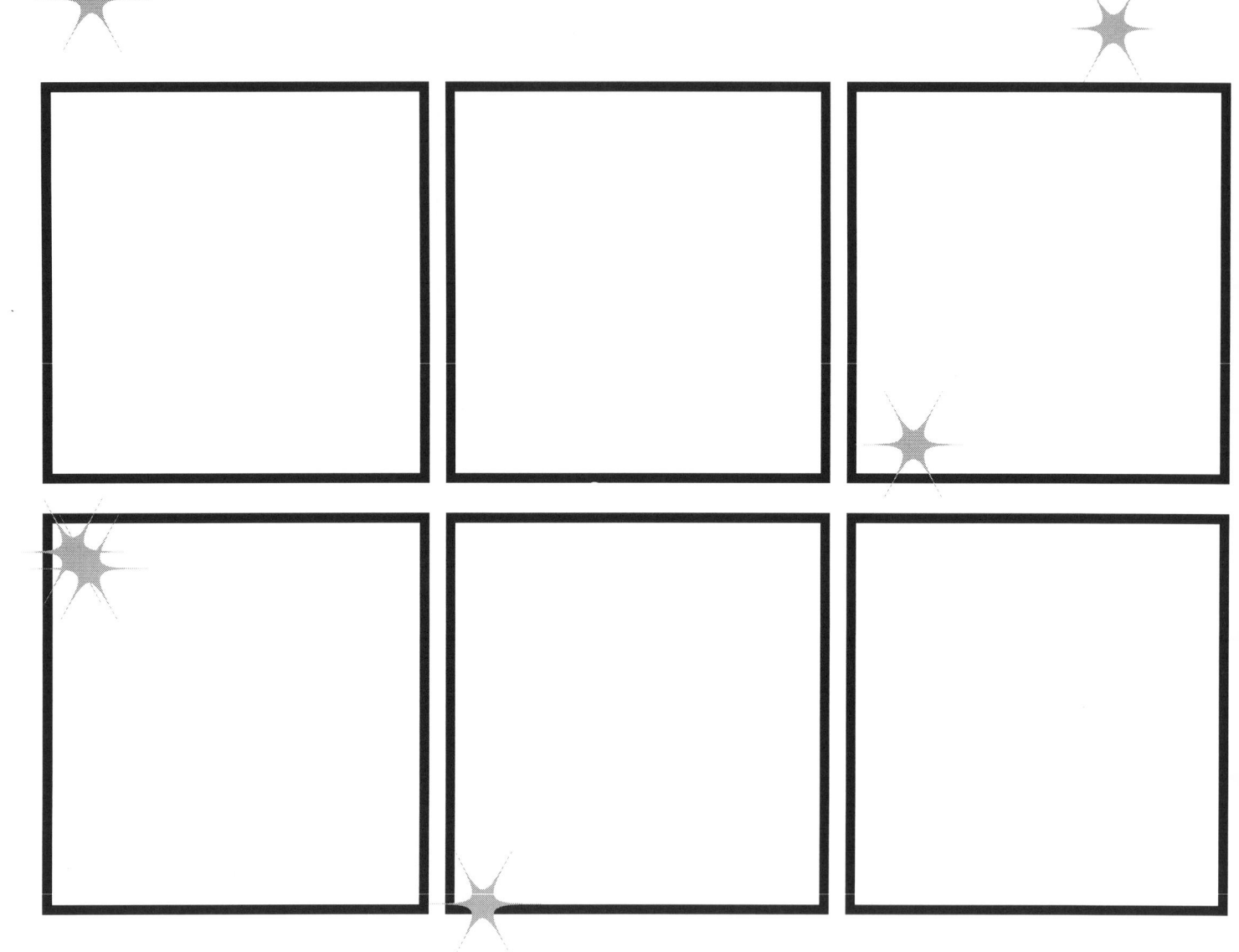

Tip: Don't limit helpful ideas to these pages, consider grabbing a real sticky note pad. Add these solutions to your mirror, bedside table, workstation, car console, kitchen cabinet, or any location that helps remind you that you ARE overcoming!

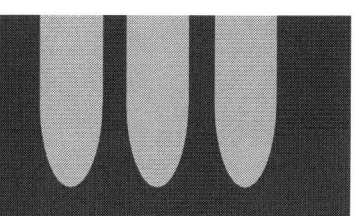

> "When you're in a Slump,
> you're not in for much fun.
> Un-slumping yourself
> is not easily done."
> — Dr. Seuss, Oh, The Places You'll Go!

THE "PS" OF ANXIETY	OVERCOMING STRATEGIES
Predictability	Define success and failure. Create a list or vision board of what you define as success. Focus on accomplishing and creating what you want, over what you fear and don't want.
Permission	Give yourself permission to feel what you are feeling, and then let go to move on. Label it, recognize the physical sensations, and scale it. Feel, breathe, and release. Scale again and repeat until the accepted emotion has passed.
Perception	Is it true? Is there another way to consider it? How might someone else in your situation see it? How do others view it?
Perfectionism	Consider "good enough" as a concept. Who is watching, judging, expecting? Consider your choices and your values.
Pessimism	Recognize catastrophic, negative only, try to think LESS negatively by asking. What is accurate? Can you find a silver lining? Can you shift anything to gratitude?
Prevention	What is the outcome of worry/anxiety? Is it helpful? How does it impact you?

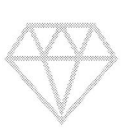

Sticky Solutions

The first step toward change is awareness.
Which "Ps" are a struggle for you?

> "The more that you read, the more things you will know. The more that you learn, the more places you'll go."
>
> -Dr. Seuss I Can Read with My Eyes Shut!

THE "PS" OF ANXIETY	OVERCOMING STRATEGIES
Present	Stay in the here and now. Avoid ruminating on the past and creating stories about the future. Consider your present options, situation, and needs.
Physical Impact	Connect with your body. What are you noticing? Where is the pain, discomfort, or tension? What can you do to release, care, and relax?
Preoccupation	Lean into the uncertainty you experience. Remind yourself: 1. I do not have to have a plan 2. I do not have to know. (answer, outcome)
Personal Responsibility	What can you control? What do you not have control over? How can you use your influence? Who/what is influencing you?
Plenty	What am you fearful is in short supply? What do you have plenty of now? What can you share? What can you invest? What is the fear?
Prayer/Meditation	Do you need to release this in prayer? Can you picture this leaving your mind, thoughts, body, and life? What might improve if you let go?

TOOLS

Be on the lookout for the tools that are useful for overcoming! Not every tool works for everyone, begin to assemble your favorites.

Looking at each of the Ps of anxiety, what are you noticing? Consider writing a few problems you face that might need a sticky solution. Be free to explore and reflect. Some boxes may be full, other boxes may be empty. Consider your unique experiences and needs.

THE PS OF ANXIETY	HOW THIS IMPACTS ME
Predictability	
Permission	
Perception	
Perfectionism	
Pessimism	
Prevention	
Present	
Physical Impact	
Preoccupation	
Personal Responsibility	
Plenty	
Prayer/Meditation	
Other	

Sticky Solution: "Being afraid is not the same as being in danger."

"Hope is the belief that something good may happen,
and the intent to make it so."
-Heather Lambert

Predictability: Finding Hope

"I might fail!" Our brains often lead us to consider that we might fail so that we are not too let down or too devastated if we do fail. Most of us have experienced failure. This is why HOPE is so important. Hope tells us to avoid predicting failure and consider other options. Our HOPES deserve space for consideration and planning.

We have experienced many obstacles to even beginning our pursuit of our goals, dreams, and desires. What is holding you back? What if you began to notice those obstacles and consider replacing them with another option, a hope? Let's practice now.

HOPES	OBSTACLE	OVERCOMING STRATEGY

Predicting happens in our thoughts, sometimes even unaware. Practicing mindfulness can help us become more aware of our metacognitions, so we can shift from predicting failure to choosing to believe and hope!

MINDFULNESS: Are you mindful or is your mind full?
Let's spend some time practicing mindfulness.

1st: Draw symbols or words that represent the thoughts that are filling your head right now.

2nd Circle any thoughts that help you feel better.

3rd Use your eraser to remove any thoughts that make you feel worse. (if you cannot erase, scratch the thought out until you can no longer see it at all)

4th Practice reminding yourself by saying, "I get to decide what I think about!" Say this three times as you focus on your favorite thoughts.

5th Is there anything you would like to add to the drawing to make you feel even better? If so, add it now.

6th Look at what you did! Tell yourself "I can control my thoughts!" Notice how your body feels as you read and breathe in all the things you like to think about.

Yes, you can!

Permission

Have there been dream squashers in your life? Did you believe them? Do you sometimes still hear their damaging words, saying, "You can't!"? What dreams, once squashed, are you ready to give yourself permission to consider again?

Squashed Dream #1:

Squashed Dream #2:

Squashed Dream #3:

Sticky Solution: " I can take the lid off my dream box!"

SKILL BUILDING: EMOTIONAL REGULATION. IT IS AS EASY AS 1-2-3-4.

① Label any sensations you are experiencing in your body. Feel free to use, colors, stickers, shapes, words, or symbols.

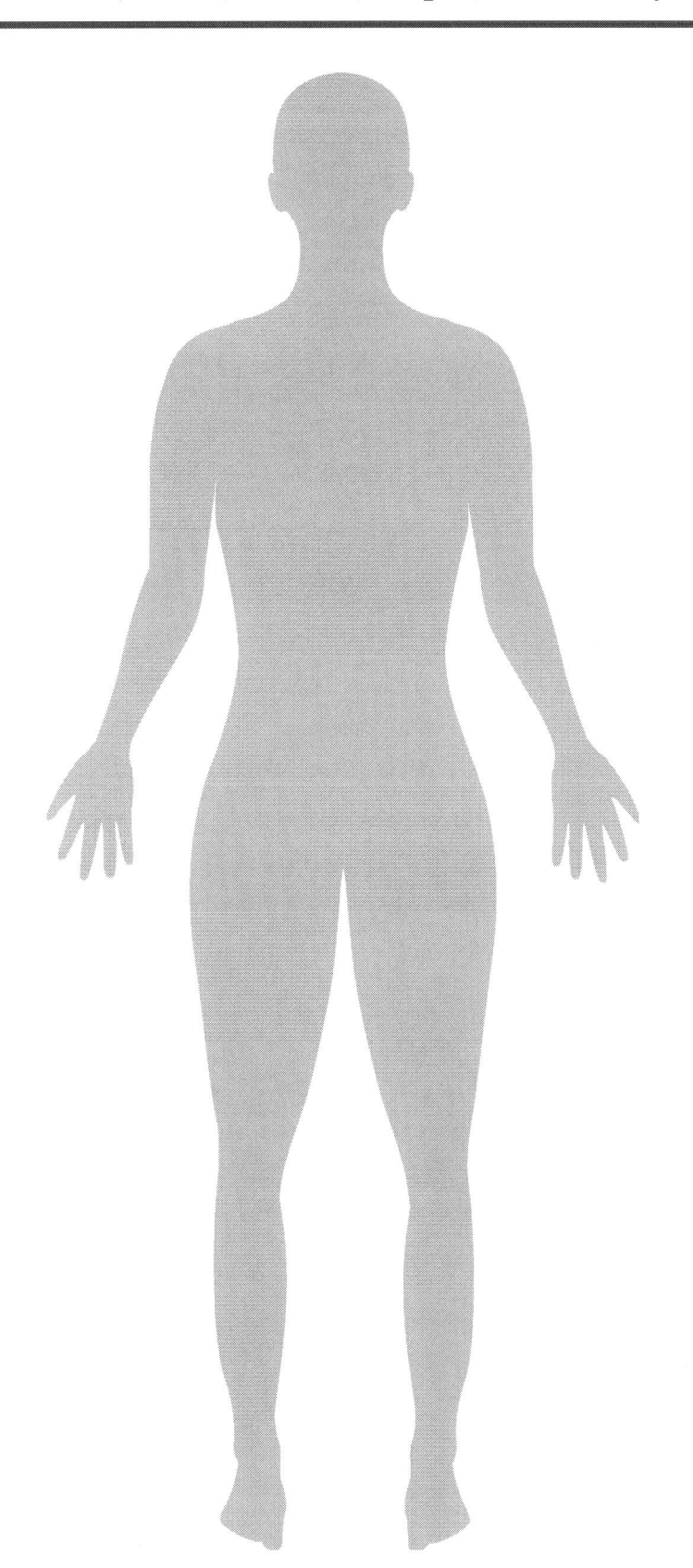

EMOTIONAL REGULATION

17

SKILL BUILDING: EMOTIONAL REGULATION. IT IS AS EASY AS 1-2-3-4.

(2) Label the emotion. As you consider the sensation, what is the label that best describes the experience? Refer to your Step 1 Body Map and replace the sensations with emotional labels. Refer to the box on the next page for help with labels.

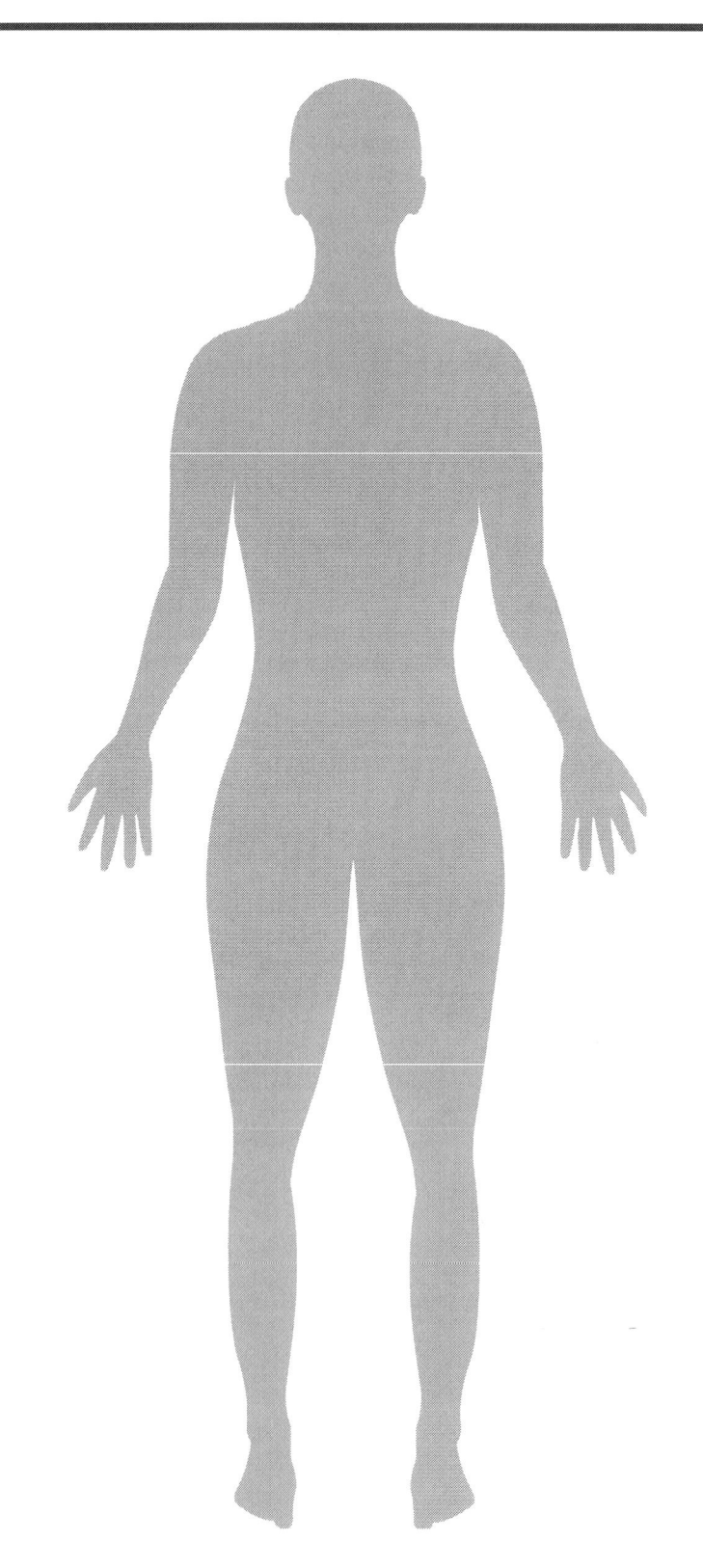

EMOTIONAL REGULATION

Feelings Sensations

hoffman
when you're serious about change

Feelings List

Accepting / Open
Calm
Centered
Content
Fulfilled
Patient
Peaceful
Present
Relaxed
Serene
Trusting

Aliveness / Joy
Amazed
Awe
Bliss
Delighted
Eager
Ecstatic
Enchanted
Energized
Engaged
Enthusiastic
Excited
Free
Happy
Inspired
Invigorated
Lively
Passionate
Playful
Radiant
Refreshed
Rejuvenated
Renewed
Satisfied
Thrilled
Vibrant

Angry / Annoyed
Agitated
Aggravated
Bitter
Contempt
Cynical
Disdain
Disgruntled
Disturbed
Edgy
Exasperated
Frustrated
Furious
Grouchy
Hostile
Impatient
Irritated
Irate
Moody
On edge
Outraged
Pissed
Resentful
Upset
Vindictive

Courageous / Powerful
Adventurous
Brave
Capable
Confident
Daring
Determined
Free
Grounded
Proud
Strong
Worthy
Valiant

Connected / Loving
Accepting
Affectionate
Caring
Compassion
Empathy
Fulfilled
Present
Safe
Warm
Worthy

Curious
Engaged
Exploring
Fascinated
Interested
Intrigued
Involved
Stimulated

Despair / Sad
Anguish
Depressed
Despondent
Disappointed
Discouraged
Forlorn
Gloomy
Grief
Heartbroken
Hopeless
Lonely
Longing
Melancholy
Sorrow
Teary
Unhappy
Upset
Weary
Yearning

Disconnected / Numb
Aloof
Bored
Confused
Distant
Empty
Indifferent
Isolated
Lethargic
Listless
Removed
Resistant
Shut Down
Uneasy
Withdrawn

Embarrassed / Shame
Ashamed
Humiliated
Inhibited
Mortified
Self-conscious
Useless
Weak
Worthless

Fear
Afraid
Anxious
Apprehensive
Frightened
Hesitant
Nervous
Panic
Paralyzed
Scared
Terrified
Worried

Fragile
Helpless
Sensitive

Grateful
Appreciative
Blessed
Delighted
Fortunate
Grace
Humbled
Lucky
Moved
Thankful
Touched

Guilt
Regret
Remorseful
Sorry

Hopeful
Encouraged
Expectant
Optimistic
Trusting

Powerless
Impotent
Incapable
Resigned
Trapped
Victim

Tender
Calm
Caring
Loving
Reflective
Self-loving
Serene
Vulnerable
Warm

Stressed / Tense
Anxious
Burned out
Cranky
Depleted
Edgy
Frazzled
Overwhelm
Rattled
Rejecting
Restless
Shaken
Tight
Weary
Worn out

Unsettled / Doubt
Apprehensive
Concerned
Dissatisfied
Disturbed
Grouchy
Hesitant
Inhibited
Perplexed
Questioning
Rejecting
Reluctant
Shocked
Skeptical
Suspicious
Ungrounded
Unsure
Worried

Body Sensations

Achy	Contracted	Gentle	Numb	Shaky	Sweaty
Airy	Dizzy	Hard	Pain	Shivery	Tender
Blocked	Drained/Exhausted	Heavy	Pounding	Slow	Tense
Breathless	Dull	Hollow	Prickly	Smooth	Throbbing
Bruised	Electric	Hot	Pulsing	Soft	Tight
Burning	Empty	Icy	Queasy	Sore	Tingling
Buzzy	Expanded	Itchy	Radiating	Spacey	Trembly
Clammy	Flowing	Jumpy	Relaxed	Spacious	Twitchy
Clenched	Fluid	Knotted	Releasing	Sparkly	Vibrating
Cold	Fluttery	Light	Rigid	Stiff	Warm
Constricted	Frozen	Loose	Sensitive	Still	Wobbly
Contained	Full	Nauseous	Settled	Suffocated	Wooden

Adapted from "Nonviolent Communication" by Marshall B. Rosenberg, Ph.D.   Rev. 06/24

Used with permission www.hoffmaninstitute.org

SKILL BUILDING: EMOTIONAL REGULATION. IT IS AS EASY AS 1-2-3-4

③ <u>Scale the emotion.</u> Consider the intensity, assign a number to the level of intensity. Use the tools below to help assess.

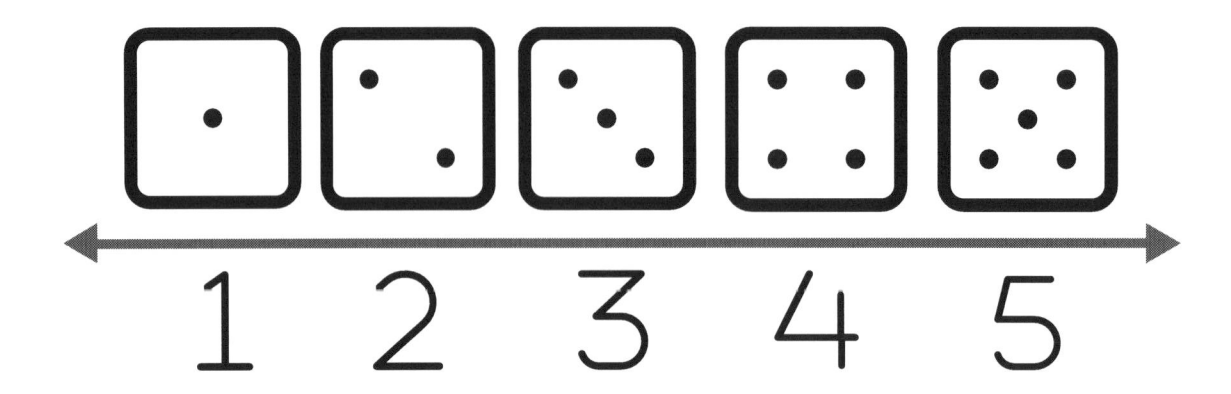

1   2   3   4   5

Emotional Sensation Scale

<u>Very Low/Minimal</u> Emotional Sensation:

Description: Barely noticeable emotional experience. Emotions are faint and hard to detect or describe. Examples: Subtle feelings of calmness, slight unease, mild disinterest.

<u>Low/Mild</u> Emotional Sensation:

Description: Noticeable but not intense. Emotions are mild and easy to tolerate without significant impact. Examples: Mild happiness, slight sadness, gentle anxiety, light amusement.

<u>Moderate</u> Emotional Sensation:

Description: Clearly noticeable and distinct. Emotions are strong enough to draw attention but not overwhelming. Examples: Moderate joy, clear frustration, noticeable sadness, moderate excitement.

<u>High/Strong</u> Emotional Sensation:

Description: Very noticeable and intense. Emotions are strong and might require conscious effort to manage. Examples: Strong happiness, intense anger, deep sadness, high anxiety.

<u>Very High/Extreme</u> Emotional Sensation:

Description: Extremely intense and possibly overwhelming. Emotions are powerful and may be difficult to tolerate or control. Examples: Euphoria, extreme rage, profound grief, severe panic.

SKILL BUILDING: EMOTIONAL REGULATION. IT IS AS EASY AS 1-2-3-4.

④ Soothe the emotion. When you have experienced, expressed, and respected the emotion, prepare to soothe or calm yourself. These steps, sometimes called *sensory soothing*, can help.

Step Four: Soothe the emotion

> Can I look at something soothing?
> A family photograph, a favorite video, a sunset.

> Can I listen to something soothing?
> A song on my phone, the clicking of the clock, the tapping of my foot.

> Can I smell something soothing?
> A candle, essential oil, a scented pencil.

> Can I taste something soothing?
> A piece of candy, a melting piece of chocolate, a drink of cool water.

> Can I feel something soothing?
> A weighted blanked, a smooth rock, a pop it fidget.

> Feel, breathe, and release.

EMOTIONAL REGULATION

1. Locate the Sensation
2. Name the Emotion
3. Scale the Emotion
4. Soothe the Emotion

Sticky Solution:

- ☐ Locate the sensation
- ☐ Soothe the emotion
- ☐ Name the emotion
- ☐ Scale the emotion
- ☐ Sooth the emotion
- ☐ Repeat as needed

Notes:

_____
_____
_____
_____
_____
_____

GOING ON A
snipe hunt

Perception: *You find what you are looking for*

A **snipe hunt is a** fool's errand pranksters ask gullible "hunters" to join. This can be just like hunting for perfectionism. Let's look for the snipes you have been pursuing!

Who do you think is "perfect"? This can be someone in your life, family, friend, social media, famous person?
_____
_____
_____
_____
_____
_____

What is their life like that your life is missing?
_____
_____
_____
_____
_____

What is it possible that you don't see about their life? (difficulty, pain, struggle, challenges)
_____
_____
_____
_____
_____

Are there things you **admire** about them and their life? How can this **inspire** you? _____
_____
_____
_____

23

Perfectionism

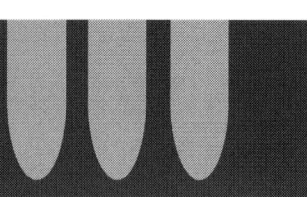

THOUGHT	OPPOSITE	MIDDLE
T	O	M

LIST A PERFECTIONIST THOUGHT YOU HAVE HAD IN THE LAST FEW DAYS.

WHAT IS THE OPPOSITE OF THAT THOUGHT?

WHAT IDEA FALLS BETWEEN THE PERFECTIONISTIC THOUGHT AND THE OPPOSITE THAT YOU CAN ACCCEPT? (MIDDLE)

EXAMPLE:

Thought. No one likes me.
Opposite: Everyone likes me
Middle: Some people like me. I know Angela, Shelly, and Tara like me. I also know Stacy, Susan, and Barbara don't like me.
Acceptance: I can accept that some people like me and some people don't.

Emotional Circuits

Each emotion in our brain connects to an opposite emotion. The most regulated emotions fall between the extremes. We can emotionally regulate by pendulating to the opposite end of the emotional circuit.

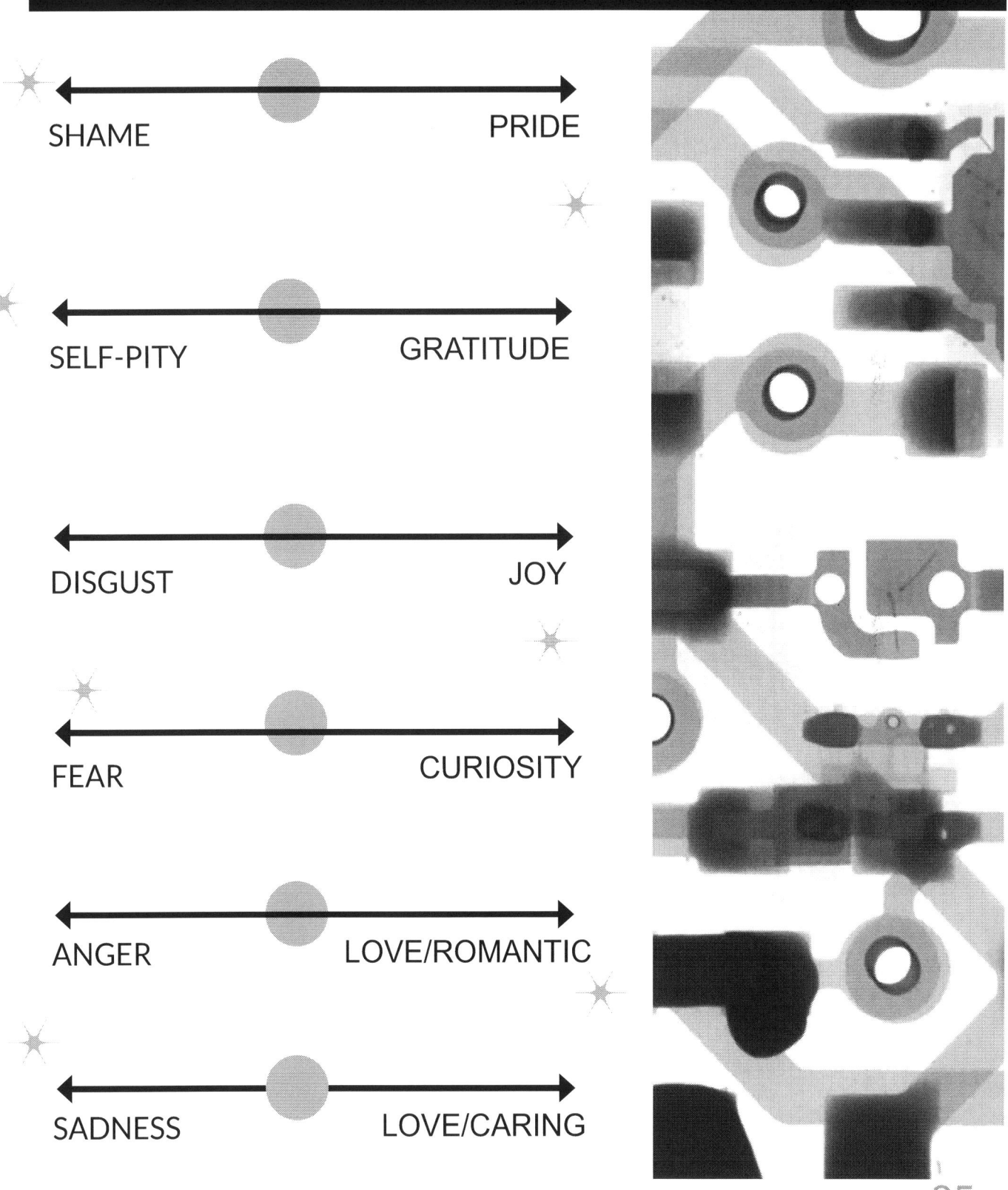

SHAME ⟷ PRIDE

SELF-PITY ⟷ GRATITUDE

DISGUST ⟷ JOY

FEAR ⟷ CURIOSITY

ANGER ⟷ LOVE/ROMANTIC

SADNESS ⟷ LOVE/CARING

Emotional Circuits

Each emotion in our brain connects to an opposite emotion. The most regulated emotions fall between the extremes. We can emotionally regulate by pendulating to the opposite end of the emotional circuit.

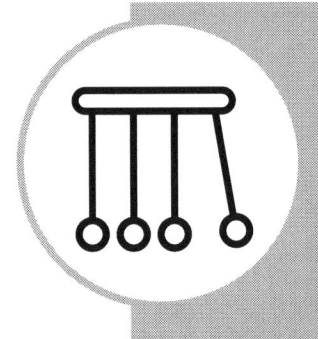

self-limiting	moderate	self-inflating
shame	sorry, regret	pride
self-pity	acceptance	gratitude
disgust	play	joy
fear	consider	curiosity
anger	openness	love/romance
sadness	kindness	love/care

Adapted from Katie O'Shea, MS and Lisa Hayes, MSW 4/16 Updating Brain Circuits

Pessimism: Stinking Thinking
Check all that apply.

✓	Thinking Error	Description	Example
○	All or Nothing Thinking	Black and white, perfectionism, few options, seeing failure	"If I don't know all the answers, I am stupid."
○	Overgeneralization — Labeling or mislabeling	Pessimism, stereotyping	"I can't draw. I am not good at anything."
○	Mental Filter	Fixations, obsessive negative thinking	"I Know I got the promotion, but it is just because I have been here the longest."
○	Disqualifying the Positive	Positive doesn't count, focus on negative	"That A doesn't count because everyone got an A in the easy class."
○	Jumping to Conclusions	Ignoring Facts to apply negative frame of thinking	"I completed the marathon, but anyone can do that."
○	Mind Reading	Believing you know what others are thinking and it is negative	This teacher doesn't like me.
○	Fortune Teller	Anticipating, predicting a negative outcome	That relationship wouldn't end well.
○	Catastrophizing	Magnifying the negative to overshadow any positive	I am going to lose my job because of this mistake.
○	Minimizing	Downplaying the positive to highlight the negative. Dismissing feelings as invalid or unimportant.	I finished the race, but I stopped and walked three times. I crossed the finish line a loser.
○	Emotional Reasoning	Using negative emotions to explain a situation	I feel uneasy, something really bad is about to happen.
○	Personalization	Making everything negative about oneself, accepting the blame	It rained and the parade was cancelled because I washed my car.
○	"Should" statements	Believing fixed rules and expectations must be met	I should have been able to keep my parents together.

Gratitude Practices

Look at the list below, select one or two gratitude practices to try this week! Notice how you feel when you pendulate from pessimism to gratitude.

◆◆◆◆◆◆◆◆◆◆◆◆◆◆◆◆◆◆◆◆◆◆

Prayers of Thanksgiving: Before meals or bed, allow yourself to feel thankful for what you recognize as goodness.
Gratitude Journal: Write something you are thankful for each day.
Say Thank You: Recognize and acknowledge kindness and goodness from others.
Give a Compliment: Look for opportunities to notice goodness in others and state it.
Nature: Connect with and notice the beauty in nature on walks, in the sunsets, in the parks, etc.
Gratitude Meditation: Clear the whiteboard in your mind. Write one thing you are thankful for and notice it. Trace it over, make it darker, color it, and add symbols or artwork.
Sensing Gratitude: Go through each of your senses, noticing something you are grateful you saw, heard, smelled, tasted, and felt.
Others: Send a friend or relative a word of kind acknowledgment for what they mean to you via text or email.
Smile: Remind your face to lighten up, lift your eyebrows, let your lips turn upward, and feel the smile.
Gratitude Jar: Create one or buy one, pull out a gratitude prompt, and answer it aloud, connecting it with the card's intent.
Plan: Get something you enjoy and can look forward to on the calendar. Remind yourself it is coming. (vacation, date, movie, dinner with a friend, visit to a park).

Gratitude Practices

Look at the list below, select one or two gratitude practices to try this week! Notice how you feel when you pendulate from pessimism to gratitude.

◆◆◆◆◆◆◆◆◆◆◆◆◆◆◆◆◆◆◆◆◆◆

Volunteer: Helping others can create a felt sense of gratitude for you.

Reward Yourself: Buy yourself a treat, nap, or get a manicure or massage because you are working hard to overcome the negative.

Write a Note: Write an old-fashioned note, get a stamp, and mail it!

Admire: Think of someone or something you admire. Let yourself feel grateful for that person or thing.

Rituals: Create a bedtime, morning, or noon ritual where you stop to think of one person or thing you are thankful for.

Learn: Watch a gratitude video or read a gratitude book. You can learn gratitude!

Tune Out: Notice the negative input (videos, social media, friends). Be grateful you can tune out the negative and focus on the positive, practice this! Unfollow, unfriend, unsubscribe, unlike, clean up your feeds.

Cook: Prepare a healthy or favorite meal. Eat it, practicing mindful eating and gratefulness.

No Complaining Rule: Set one hour or pick one day to avoid complaining and negativity. Instead, replace it with the intention to be grateful.

Notice Others: Thank those who wait on you, clean your offices, drive your Uber, pick up your trash, etc.

Post-it Note: Leave an encouraging thought on a post-it note in the restroom, mailroom, classroom, hallway, or bus stop. You can BE the encouragement for others; it is sticky!

Health Benefits of Gratitude

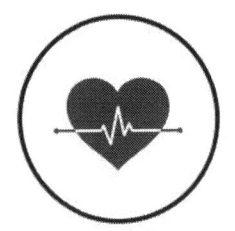

- Lower risk of heart disease, diabetes, some cancers and other lifestyle diseases
- Stronger immune system 
- Sharper memory and less mental decline with aging 
- Higher-quality sleep and less insomnia 
- Reduced perception of chronic pain 
- Less inflammation in the body 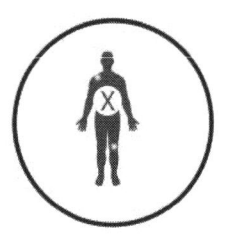
- Better mood and less incidence of depression and anxiety 
- Higher self-confidence and fewer feelings of anger, jealousy and envy 
- Greater ability to forgive yourself and others 
- Better ability to prioritize and manage time 

What benefits of gratitude are you enjoying?

_____
_____
_____
_____
_____
_____
_____

Prevention: Locus of Control

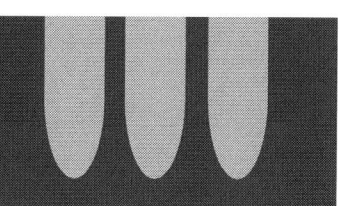

INTERNAL LOCUS OF CONTROL.
I am in control. I make things happen.

EXTERNAL LOCUS OF CONTROL.
I have no control. Things happen to me.

Remember TOM? Thought, Opposite, Middle?
An out-of-balance locus of control requires a move toward the middle. While we have learned it is unhealthy to have a pessimistic, negative outlook, we have also learned it is unhealthy to have a perfectionistic, controlling viewpoint. A healthy realization is there are some things we can control and some we cannot.

3 THINGS I CAN CONTROL ARE:

1.

3 THINGS I CANNOT CONTROL ARE:

2.

3 THINGS I CAN INFLUENCE ARE:

3.

You've got to know when to hold 'em
Know when to fold 'em
Know when to walk away
And know when to run
The Gambler, Kenny Rogers

"Yesterday is history, tomorrow is a mystery, but today is a gift. That's why it's called the present" - unknown

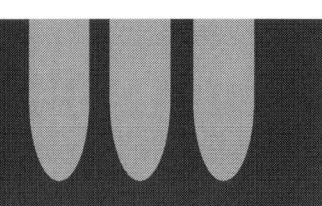

Practicing Being Present

The past can be a source of regret, sorrow, and even depression.

The present has the opportunity for many emotions, experiences, expressions, or needs. Remaining IN the present ensures you are focused on what is happening and exercising your locus of control.

Going too far forward can cause you to lose the present and can increase:

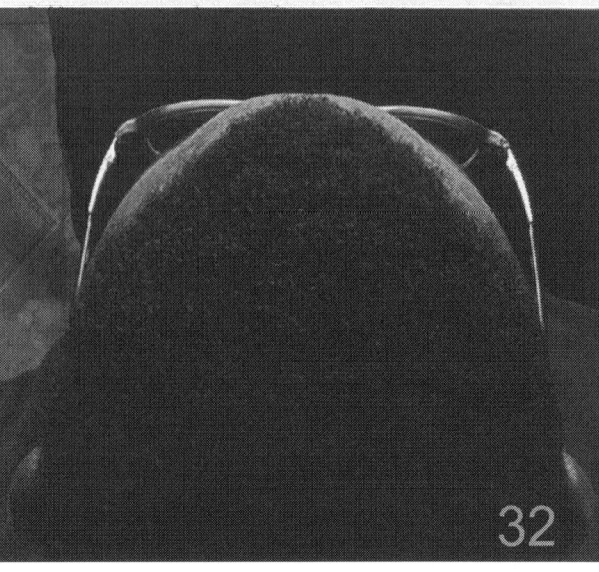

- anxiety
- anticipatory grief
- "storying" or planning stressful scenarios

Staying Grounded

Sensory Grounding Techniques to Stay in the Present

Sight	Smell	Taste	Hear	Feel
Look at a picture book or magazine	Light a candle	Place a piece of chocolate or another favorite treat in your mouth, don't chew it, notice it melting and feel the flavors	Listen to your breathe as you breathe in your nose and out your mouth	Put your hands in water, change the temperature from warm to cool
Watch the sunset/sunrise, notice the colors changing	Diffuse essential oils	Take a drink of water, as you allow it to move over your tongue, what do you notice?	Listen to a favorite song	Grab a comfortable blanket, wrap yourself in it and feel your body becoming warmer
Watch the clouds moving by	Take a deep breathe, noticing and labeling the smells	Mindfully eat your favorite food, allow it to sit in your mouth a moment longer before you swallow. What do you notice?	Listen to the sounds around you, notice everything you hear. The air conditioner, heart beating, clock ticking, sounds of others	Pick up items near you, notice how they feel? Heavy, light, warm, or cool?
Breathe deeply, watch you chest rise and fall	Chew a piece of gum, or have a piece of hard candy, notice the scents	Drink an herbal tea	Hum slowly in a low tone, notice the sensations and the sounds	Hold a piece of ice, feel the change in your hand as it melts
Look at preferred photos, keep a calming photo file on your phone	Place a few drops of an essential oil on a cotton ball, put it in a small zipper bag and open it with your face near the bag take a deep breathe in through your nose, notice the scent	Eat a piece of fruit, focus on the 3 Ts: Taste Texture Temperature	Go outside, listen for nature sounds. Imagine where it is coming from, what animals do you hear?	Breathe in deeply for 3 seconds. Hold your breathe for 3 seconds. Breathe out completely for 3 seconds

clearhope training

CREATE

Creating is a great way to reduce anxiety and remain in a peaceful present. Follow these steps to create your own mandala.

Materials Needed

Paper Compass (or a circular object to trace) Ruler
Pencil
Eraser
Fine-tipped markers or colored pencils

Steps to Draw a Mandala

Find the center of your paper and mark it lightly with a pencil.

Draw the Base Circles:

Use a compass (or trace circular objects of varying sizes) to draw a series of concentric circles around the center point. You can draw as many circles as you like, depending on how detailed you want your mandala to be. For beginners, 3-5 circles are a good start.

Divide the Circles:

Using a ruler, draw lines through the center point to divide the circles into equal sections. Start with dividing the circle into 4 sections (like a cross), then divide those sections into 8, and so on. The more sections, the more complex your mandala will be.

Create Patterns:

Start adding patterns in each section of the mandala. You can use shapes like petals, dots, leaves, and geometric shapes. Begin from the innermost circle and work your way outwards. Repeat patterns in each section to maintain symmetry.

Add Details:

Continue adding details and patterns to each section. Feel free to experiment with different shapes and designs. The key is to keep the patterns symmetrical.

Ink Your Mandala:

Once you're happy with your pencil design, trace over your patterns with a fine-tipped marker. This will make your mandala more defined. Let the ink dry and then carefully erase any pencil lines that are still visible.

Color Your Mandala:

Use colored pencils, markers, or paints to color your mandala. Choose colors that appeal to you and fill in the patterns you've created.

A sample mandala:
draw, design, color, and create!

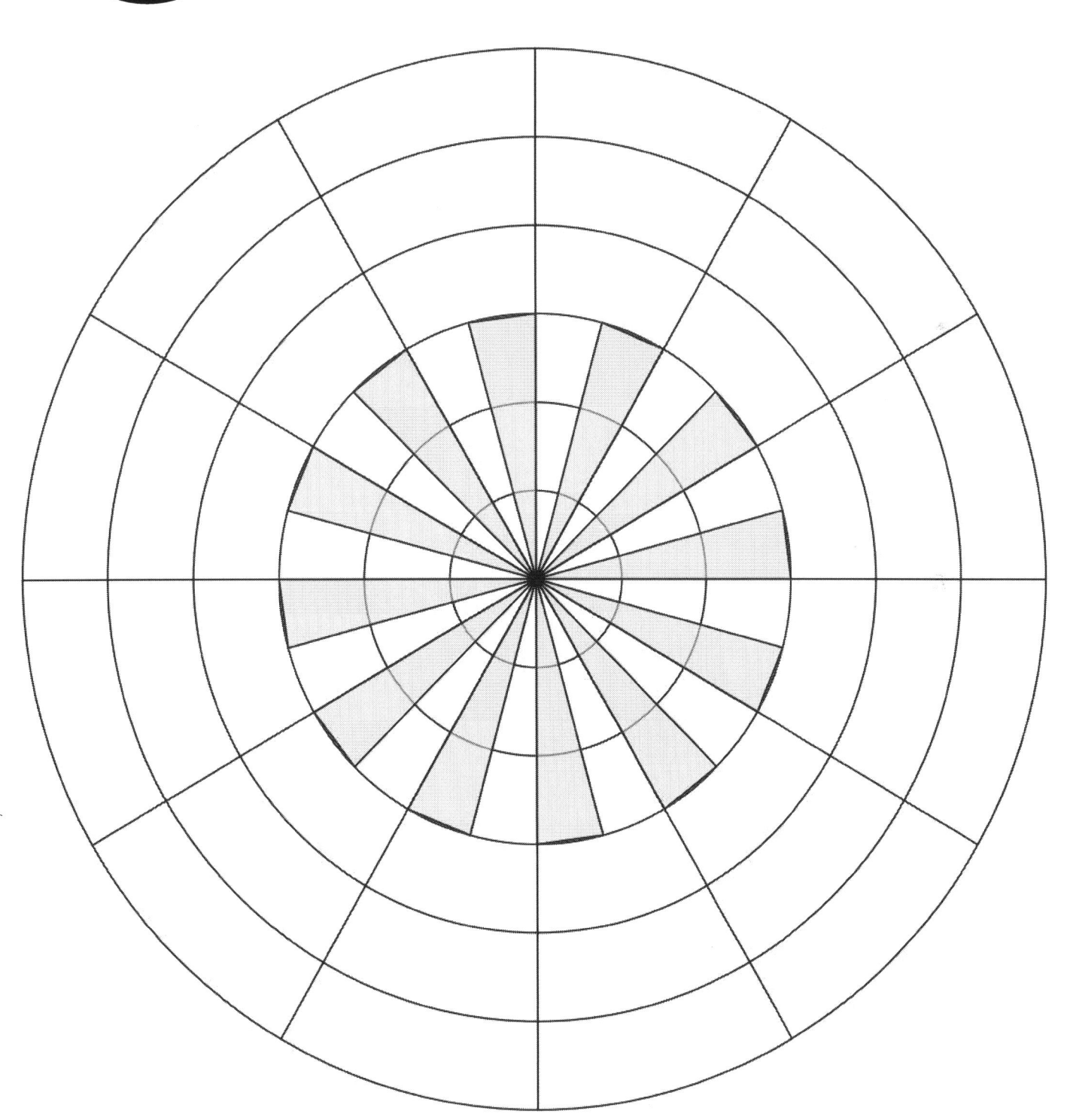

02 GAD-7
Generalized Anxiety Disorder Scale

Over the last 2 weeks, how often have you been bothered by the following problems?	Not at all	Several days	Over half the days	Nearly every day
1. Feeling nervous, anxious, or on edge	0	1	2	3
2. Not being able to stop or control worrying	0	1	2	3
3. Worrying too much about different things	0	1	2	3
4. Trouble relaxing	0	1	2	3
5. Being so restless that it is hard to sit still	0	1	2	3
6. Becoming easily annoyed or irritable	0	1	2	3
7. Feeling afraid as if something awful might happen	0	1	2	3
Add the score for each column				
Total Score (add the column scores) =				

Consider the impact of anxiety on your functioning:
How difficult have these made it for you to do your work, take care of things at home, or getting along with other people?

- ☐ Not difficult at all
- ☐ Somewhat difficult
- ☐ Very difficult
- ☐ Extremely difficult

Source: Spitzer RL, Kroenke K, Williams JBW, Lowe B. A brief measure for assessing generalized anxiety disorder. Arch Inern Med. 2006;166:1092-1097.

02 GAD-7

Generalized Anxiety Disorder Scale

Let's get a starting point as you consider your anxiety and your personal journey to overcoming. Record the total score and date of this 2nd screening. Please read and consider the disclaimers below.

Scoring GAD-7 Anxiety Severity

Total score for the 7 items ranges from 0 to 21.

- ☐ 0–4: minimal anxiety
- ☐ 5–9: mild anxiety
- ☐ 10–14: moderate anxiety
- ☐ 15–21: severe anxiety

Score:_____ Date: _____

Disclaimer: The Generalized Anxiety Disorder 7-item (GAD-7) scale is a self-administered tool designed to screen for and measure the severity of generalized anxiety disorder. While it can provide valuable insights into your anxiety levels, it is not a substitute for professional medical advice, diagnosis, or treatment.
Informational Purposes Only: The results of the GAD-7 are intended for informational and educational purposes only.
Not a Professional Assessment: This tool does not replace a comprehensive evaluation by a licensed mental health professional. Only a qualified healthcare provider can diagnose anxiety or any other mental health disorder.
Seek Professional Help: If you have concerns about your mental health or if the GAD-7 indicates high levels of anxiety, please seek advice from a healthcare provider. If you are experiencing a mental health crisis, contact emergency services immediately.
Limitations: The GAD-7 has limitations and can not capture all aspects of your mental health.

Source: Spitzer RL, Kroenke K, Williams JBW, Lowe B. A brief measure for assessing generalized anxiety disorder. Arch Inern Med. 2006;166:1092-1097.

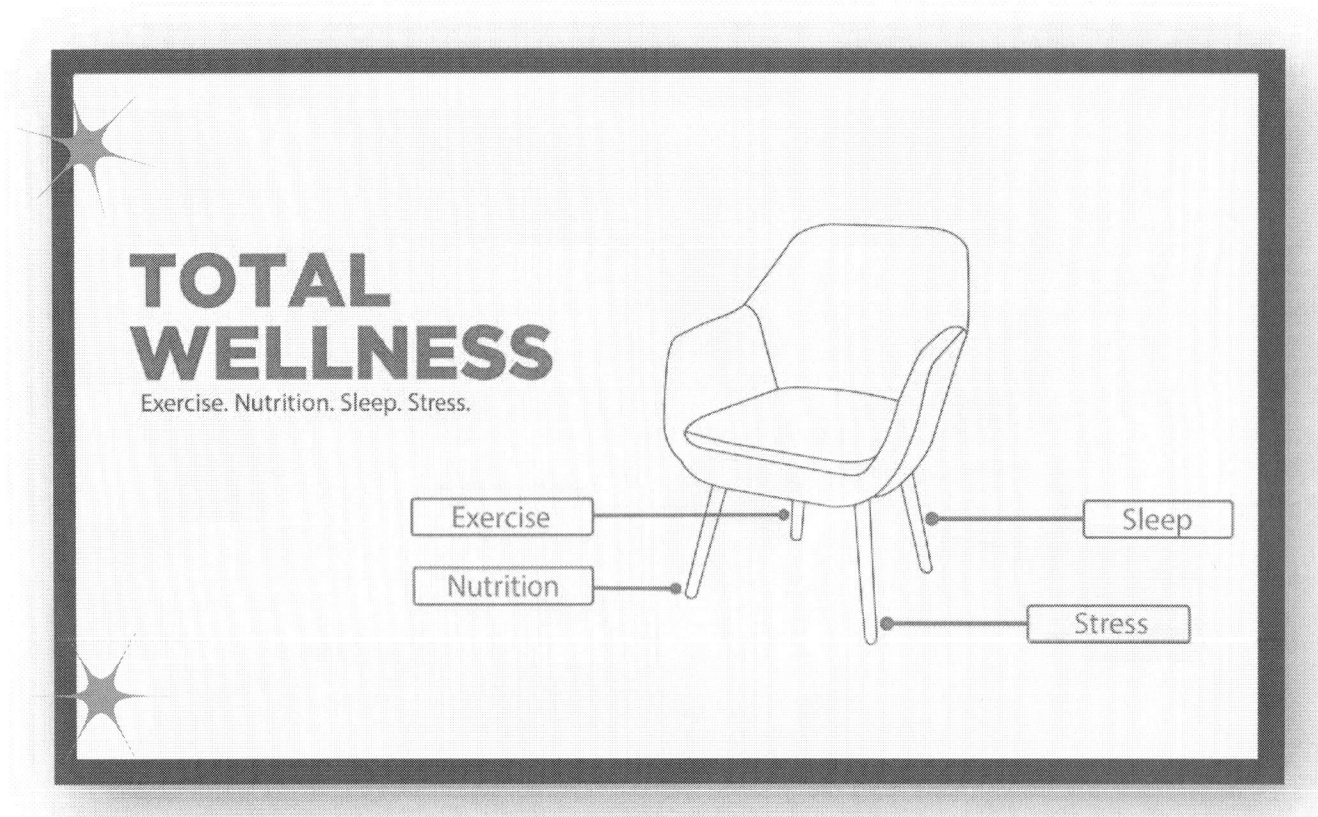

TOTAL WELLNESS
Exercise. Nutrition. Sleep. Stress.

We must take care of our bodies. This includes exercise, healthy eating, rest, and a healthy environment. We can **design our lives** by caring for our minds—and bodies.

WHERE DOES YOUR EXERCISE ROUTINE NEED A DESIGN EDIT?

WHERE DOES YOUR DIET NEED A DESIGN EDIT?

WHERE DOES YOUR SLEEP HYGIENE NEED A DESIGN EDIT?

WHERE DOES YOUR STRESS MANAGEMENT NEED A DESIGN EDIT?

Feel the Feels.

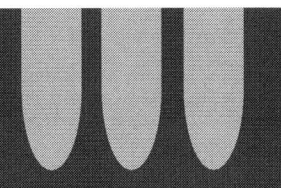

Anxiety: Body Symptoms

Irregular or increased heart rate; Trembling; Sweating, hot flashes; face flushing; Stomach pain/nausea/digestive trouble; Churning, turning, or sick feeling in the stomach; Lightheaded, dizziness; Chest pains; Headaches, body aches, pain, Weakness or tingling feeling in the limbs; Tense muscles, clenched fists; Confusion; Rashes; Pain; Clearing the throat, coughing; Changes in sex drive; Insomnia/sleep issues; Fatigue; Rapid breathing or shortness of breath; Grinding teeth/clenching jaw; Panic attacks; Increased rate of breathing

✓ Time for a check-in. What are the top 3 symptoms you are currently experiencing?

1.

2.

3.

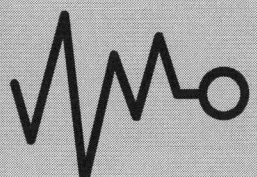

Somatization implies a tendency to experience and communicate **psychological distress** in the form of somatic symptoms and to seek medical help for them.

SCARCITY: A scarcity mindset is a belief that our resources are limited and Insufficient.

""The fear of not having enough money is actually about fearing that we are not enough." We want to find meaning and peace. We want meaningful connections. *-Kate Swoboda*

When we hold a scarcity mindset, we tend to focus on what we lack rather than what we have, which often leads to anxiety, stress, and a constant sense of not having enough.

What fears of "not enough" are causing you anxiety in these 3 key areas?

MONEY	TIME	ENERGY

Create a Financial Budget

Many budgeting tools are available online. Consider using these steps to begin to understand your spending and income.

- List how much money you earn in a given period (month, year).
- List your fixed expenses for that given period.
- Subtract your expenses from your earnings.
- If you have a surplus, decide what you want to do with the overage.
- If you have a deficit, look for ways to decrease the expenses.

*While many feel a budget is painfully restrictive, it is a path **you decide upon** to reduce your anxiety and improve your life.*

Salary		
Additional Income		
	$$$ TOTAL INCOME $$$	
Mortgage/Rent		
Groceries		
Medical Expenses/prescriptions		
Subscriptions: TV, streaming, Internet, Phone, Mobile		
Utilities: Gas, Electric, Water		
Insurances: home, car, life, health, pet, travel, other		
Debt: loans, cars, credit cards		
Investments		
Savings		
Gifts/Holidays		
Repairs/Renovations		
Other:		
Other:		
	$$TOTAL EXPENSES $$	
Subtract total expenses from total income	adjust expenses as needed: →	

Create a Time Budget (Scheduling)

Many schedules/planners are available online or in paper form. Consider using these steps to begin to understand your time and priorities.

---

1. List your total time (break this down into "plans" daily, weekly, monthly, yearly, five years, ten years, twenty years, etc.)

2. List your time commitments (these are inflexible expenditures like work, childcare, commuting, preferred time commitments, hobbies, relationships, and interests)

3. Subtract your commitments from your total time

4. Track your actual time expenditures

5. Make a new budget before the following time period begins

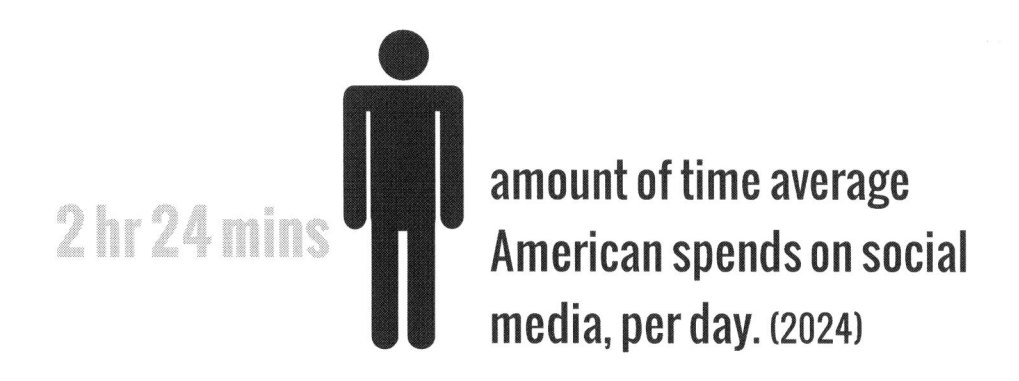

---

2 hr 24 mins — amount of time average American spends on social media, per day. (2024)

Time management has long been a struggle of humankind. The struggle can end with—you guessed it—**planning.**

Create: Priorities & Values List

How we prioritize, depends on what we value.

List your time commitments, then assign a value using the rating system.

This task is the most important task to complete in _____ (time period: today, this week, this month, this year).

① ② ③ ④ ⑤

Strongly disagree | Disagree | Equal | Agree | Strongly agree

COMMITMENTS	VALUE #
EX: Time with best friend	4

Reflecting on your commitments and values, add your priorities (in order of importance) to your ideal monthly calendar.

Designing My Life

Monthly Priorities

SUN	MON	TUE	WED	THU	FRI	SAT

"We design our lives one decision at a time."
Heather Lambert

PRIORITIES CHECK

OVERCOMING!

Our anxiety increases when our highest prioritized values get the least amount of time. Our values don't match our function. This creates cognitive dissonance.

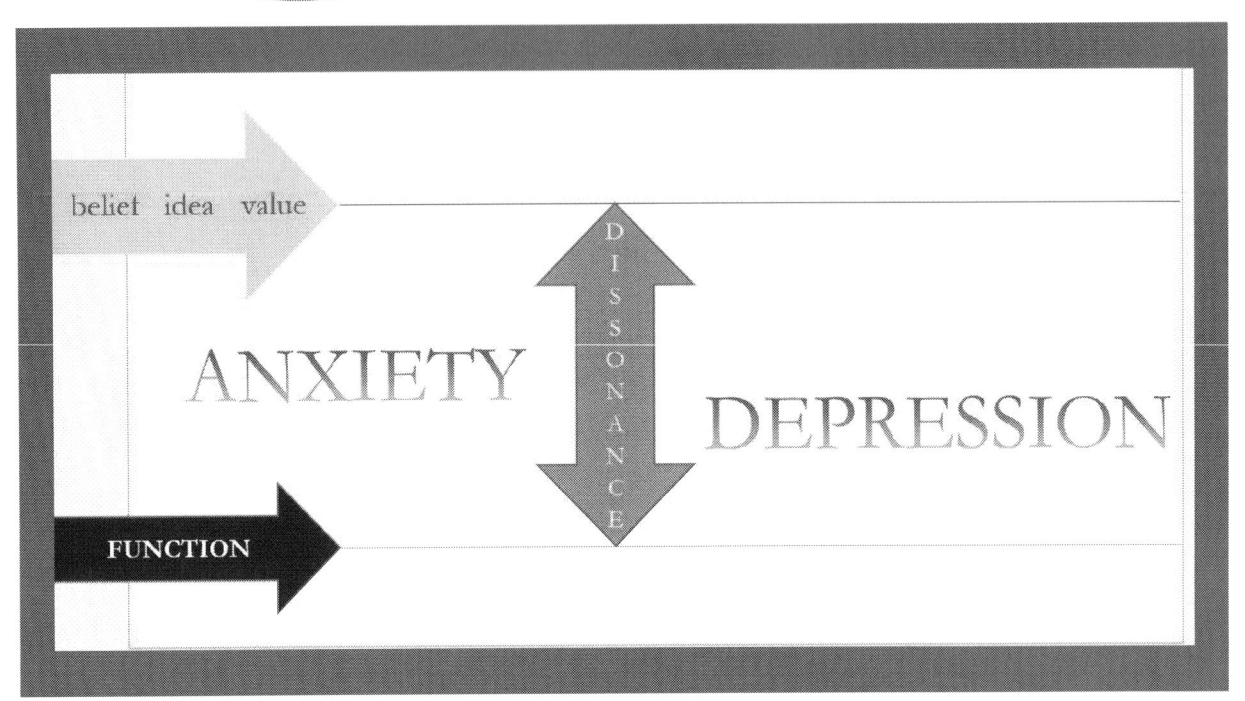

belief idea value →

ANXIETY ↕ DISSONANCE **DEPRESSION**

FUNCTION →

Where is your dissonance? _____
_____
_____
_____

What changes do you need to make? _____
_____
_____
_____
_____

TIP: To reduce dissonance, you can either change your value or change your function.

Create a Energy Budget (Spoon Theory)

Many schedules/planners are available online or in paper form. Consider using these steps to begin to understand your time and priorities.

1. List how much energy you begin within a given period (day, week). SPOONS

2. List your fixed energy expenses for that given period (commute, work tasks, relational needs).

3. Subtract your energy expenses from your energy resources.

4. If you have a surplus, decide what to do with the overage (hobbies, new work project, second job, back to school).

5. If you have a deficit, look for ways to decrease the energy expenses (boundaries, refusing to engage, caring less).

20% of workers are so burned out that they think of quitting every day. (2024)

The greatest self-care is an intentional plan for how to spend our energy.

SPOON THEORY

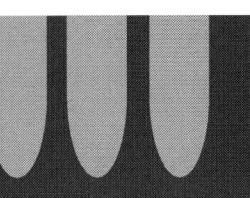

We begin each day with a limited number of "spoons" (a way to represent energy), and daily tasks require us to surrender those "spoons," so our goal is to end the day with a spoon or two left for things we enjoy instead of ending the day out of spoons, overly tired, and overspent.

DAILY TASKS	SPOONS REQUIRED

TOTAL SPOONS NEEDED

Energy Saving Solutions

- [ ] **Invisible Earmuffs:** Refuse to "listen" to things that drain your energy.
- [ ] **Refuse to Argue:** You can absolutely refuse to argue or engage in an argument with your children, significant other, or boss.
- [ ] **Take a Time Out:** If you find yourself in the middle of a relational or work demand that feels too taxing, please take a time out.
- [ ] **Get More Spoons:** Several ways exist to increase your energy supply. This can include learning new social or leadership skills. You might hire an executive functioning coach. You can begin therapy. You can find ways to laugh during the day. You can practice gratitude. You can stop and practice mindfulness, prayer, and meditation. You can practice mindful breathing, noticing, and respecting your body's needs.
- [ ] **Reframe All Advice-giving as Care:** When others share advice, we can feel judged or dismissed. An energy-protecting skill can be to receive advice as care and not feel the advice is a command. A very energy-protecting skill in response to anyone who gives advice is to say, "Thank you for caring. I'll consider that." You do not need to feel responsible for following up on your thoughts about the advice.

When we get to that place of total "spentness," we are often left with no choice but to file bankruptcy. We are literally saying, "I can't pay all my bills and still have money for the things required to live." Last breath, last dollar, last effort. Energy bankruptcy can be the scariest of all. Energy overspent is more than being burned out. An energy deficit leads to despair, the constant acknowledgment that "I can't." We cannot risk this type of deficit. What can you do to save or restore your energy?

_____
_____
_____
_____
_____
_____
_____
_____

To care best for ourselves, we must understand that our scarcity mindset comes from not respecting our limited resources.

LOOKING THROUGH A NEW LENS

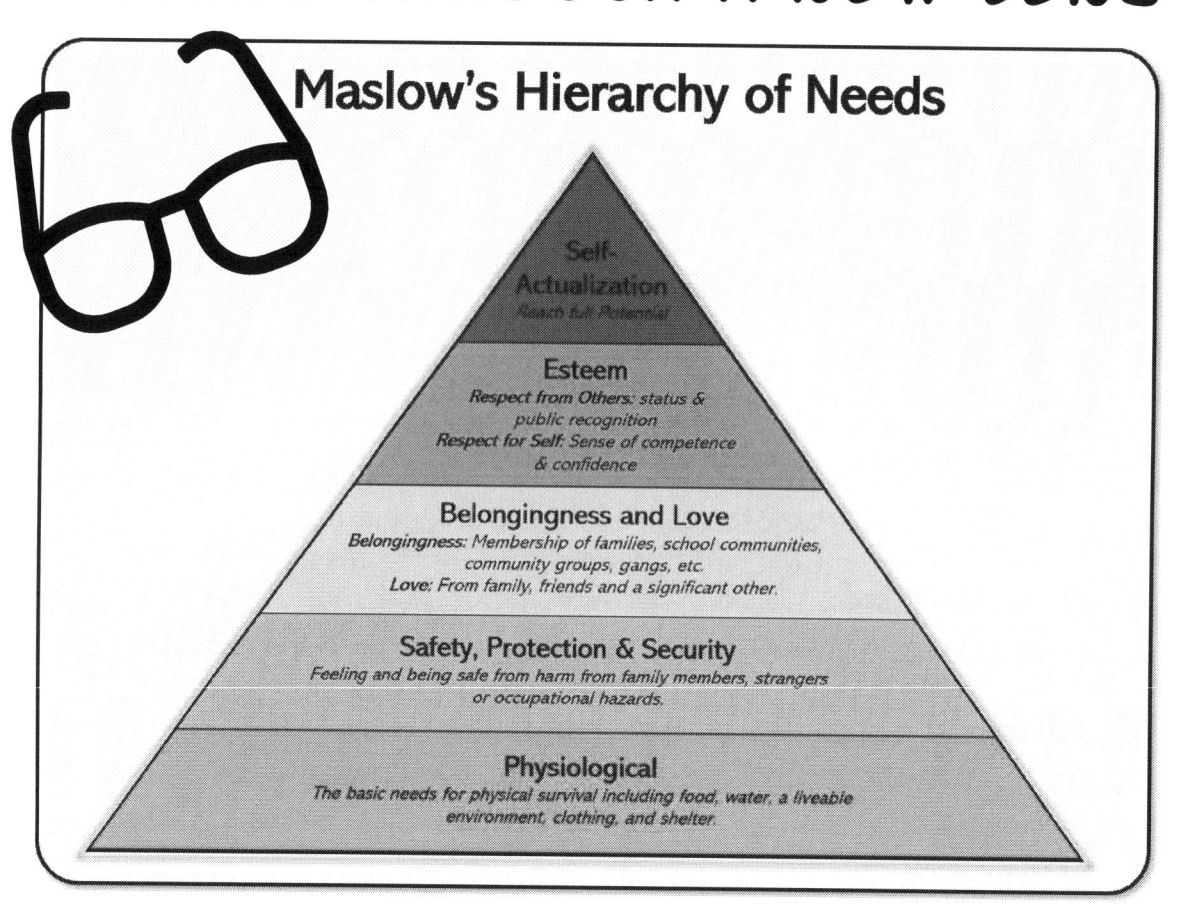

Maslow's Hierarchy of Needs

- **Self-Actualization**: Reach full Potential
- **Esteem**
  - *Respect from Others*: status & public recognition
  - *Respect for Self*: Sense of competence & confidence
- **Belongingness and Love**
  - *Belongingness*: Membership of families, school communities, community groups, gangs, etc.
  - *Love*: From family, friends and a significant other.
- **Safety, Protection & Security**
  - Feeling and being safe from harm from family members, strangers or occupational hazards.
- **Physiological**
  - The basic needs for physical survival including food, water, a liveable environment, clothing, and shelter.

We must feel safe to experience love and belonging.
Trauma can distort our view of ourselves, others, and the world around us.;
When you feel unsafe, your whole body is impacted. Your view is affected. Your functioning is impacted. Your relationships are impacted. Your performance is impacted.
Trauma has massive repercussions.

How is trauma affecting you?

_____
_____
_____
_____
_____

Where are you on Maslow's hierarchy?

_____
_____
_____
_____
_____

If we are not trauma-informed as leaders, educators, and helpers, we will contribute to the experiencer's life-long question, asking, "What is wrong with me?" We need to reframe this question. What is "wrong with me" should shift to "What happened to me?" See the difference? Instead of believing that YOU are the problem, the experiences shaped and changed you and caused problems for you.

Hope Again...

We need new neural networks. Here is a list of 21 ideas to help climb out of the physiological and safety needs focus back into the love and belonging focus.

- [ ] Consider therapy.
- [ ] Seek support from loved ones.
- [ ] Manage your finances.
- [ ] Set boundaries.
- [ ] Know your values.
- [ ] Live your values.
- [ ] Stay physically active.
- [ ] Meditate and pray.
- [ ] Reframe your thinking and gain control, working with and understanding your brain states.
- [ ] Surround yourself with people who have an abundance mindset.
- [ ] Create win-win situations.
- [ ] Practice gratitude.
- [ ] Train your mind to recognize the possibilities are endless. Find HOPE!
- [ ] Begin to dream again.
- [ ] Begin to trust again.
- [ ] Begin to believe that relationships matter.
- [ ] Remind yourself that feeling afraid is not the same as being in danger.
- [ ] Understand your trauma.
- [ ] Believe you are braver than you feel and smarter than you think.
- [ ] Give yourself some compassion. You have been through a lot
- [ ] Give others some compassion. They have been through a lot.

When we are trapped in our survival brain, fighting for physiological and safety needs, we sacrifice our belonging and esteem needs.

Peopleing: We Need Each Other!

Personal Responsibility
1. I am responsible for my thoughts, feelings, beliefs, and behaviors.
2. I am not responsible for anyone else's thoughts, feelings, beliefs, or behaviors.
3. I have influence on the thoughts, feelings, beliefs and behaviors of others.

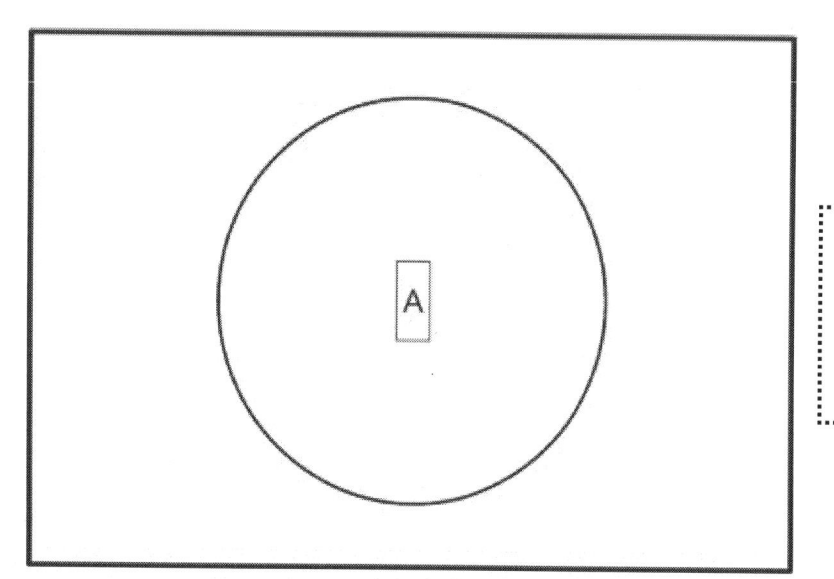

All the greatness that is you has a deep desire for connection to be in a relationship with someone else.

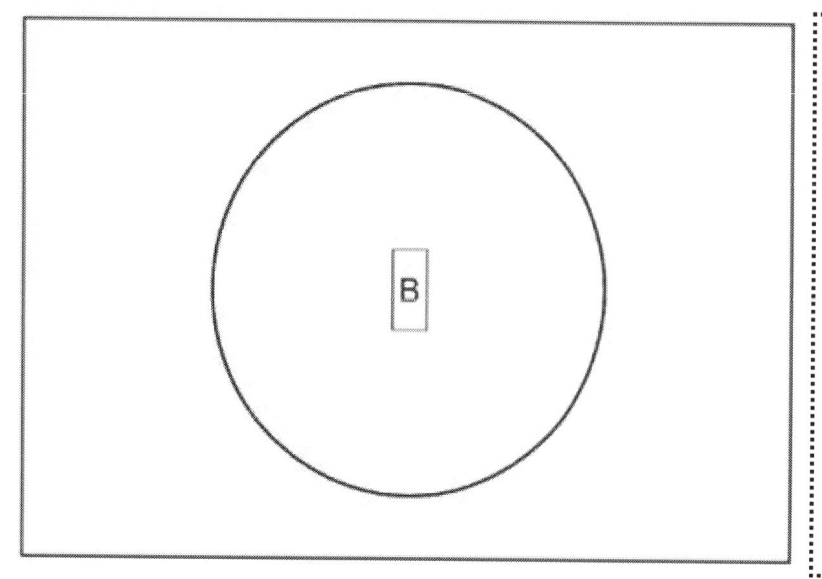

Potential candidates for a relationship with you because you have some mutual interests, abilities, or shared experiences. connections, experiences, or interests. Although you have commonalities, each is their own circle. You are each an individual. Healthy relationships are careful to maintain individuality while looking for commonality.

Peopleing: We Need Each Other!

In your relationships, consider your responsibility and care for your own:

thoughts

feelings

beliefs

behaviors

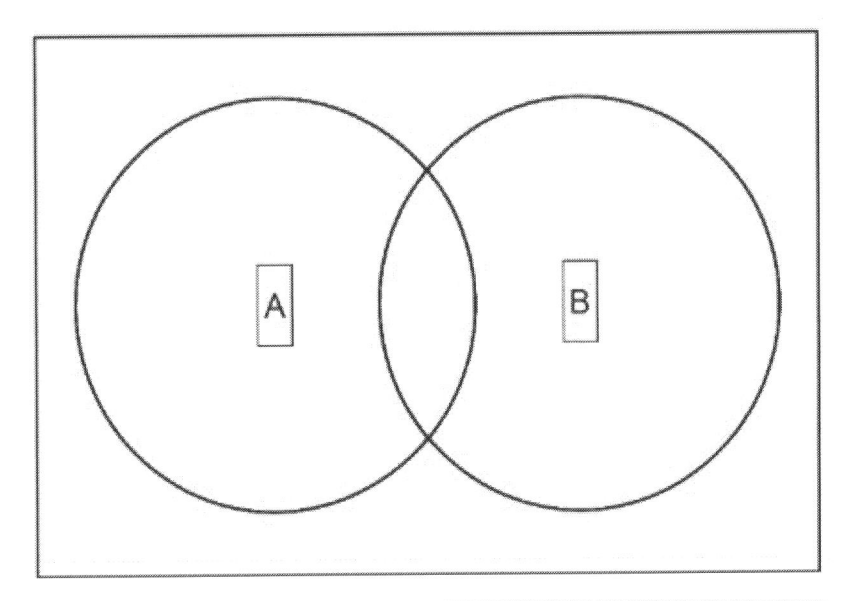

A mutually beneficial relationship based on identified similarities or shared interests or values is developed. Each person continues to have their own unique circle, A and B. Yet, the connection is obvious. The areas of overlap add meaning to the relationship, and the uniqueness also adds interest to your life.

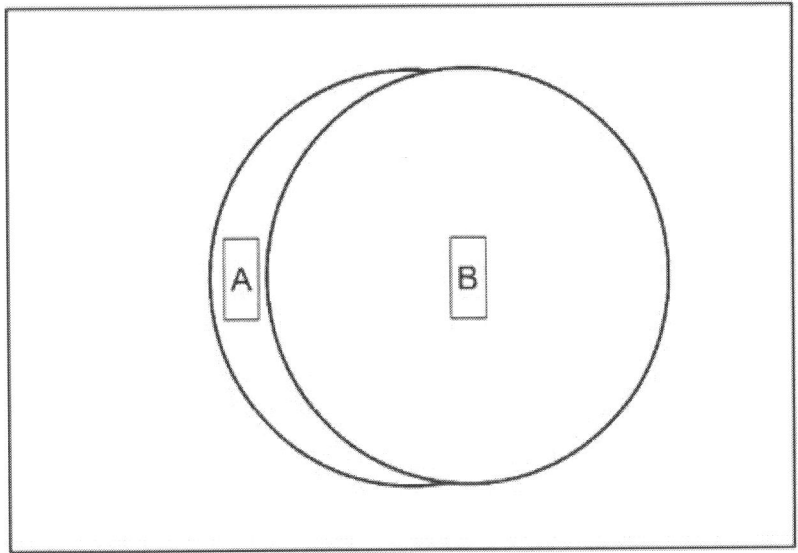

When we become fearful we may lose a relationship, we can begin people pleasing. To reduce anxiety, we work to give more of ourselves to B. Then, we lose ourselves. This can happen when we struggle with relational injuries, attachment traumas, or loss of love due to death or other difficult circumstances.

Peopleing: We Need Each Other!

In your relationships, consider how you assume the responsibility or *feel* responsible for other people's

thoughts

feelings

beliefs

behaviors

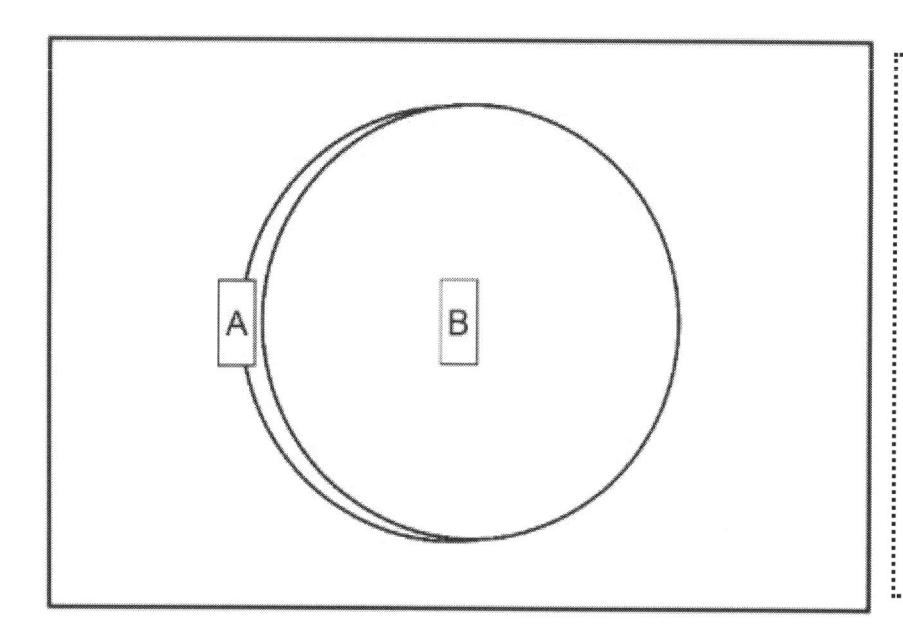

Codependency, or relationship addiction, is an emotional and behavioral condition that affects the ability to have a healthy, mutually satisfying relationship. The relationship becomes one-sided, emotionally destructive, demanding, and even abusive. Anxiety, rooted in a fear of being alone or lonely, leads us to cling to another person in unhealthy ways and to remain in relationships that are unhealthy

Healthy Relationships Require...

1. Open Communication
2. Mutual Respect
3. Kindness
4. Positive Regard
5. Time

54

Peopleing: We Need Each Other!

Personal Responsibility

1. I am responsible for my thoughts, feelings, beliefs, and behaviors.
2. I am not responsible for anyone else's thoughts, feelings, beliefs, or behaviors.
3. I have influence on the thoughts, feelings, beliefs and behaviors of others.

How would you describe your closest relationships?

When reviewing personal responsibility, do you see you struggle with appropriate boundaries?

When reviewing the **healthy relationship model 1-5** from the previous page, what areas are you experiencing in your relationships? What areas are a struggle?

Peopleing: We Need Each Other!

Make your circle BIGGER!
One of the ways to reduce anxiety and overcome codependent, enmeshed relationships is to ADD more interests, events, and people to your circle.
How can you make your circle **BIGGER**?
Think about your interests, skills, natural abilities, hobbies, character, and preferences.
What do you miss? Want to add? Want to consider?

A

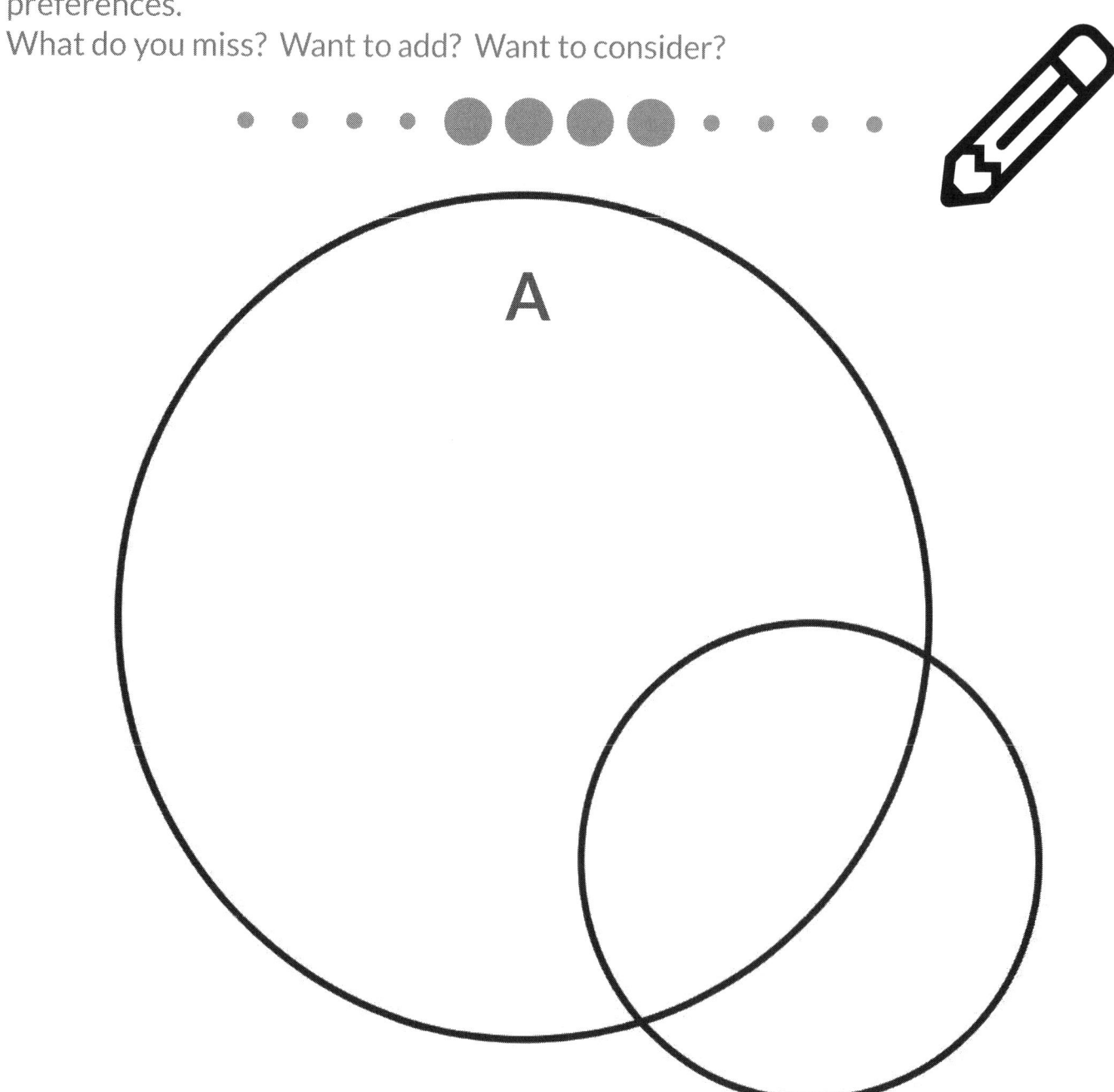

03 GAD-7
Generalized Anxiety Disorder Scale

Over the last 2 weeks, how often have you been bothered by the following problems?	Not at all	Several days	Over half the days	Nearly every day
1. Feeling nervous, anxious, or on edge	0	1	2	3
2. Not being able to stop or control worrying	0	1	2	3
3. Worrying too much about different things	0	1	2	3
4. Trouble relaxing	0	1	2	3
5. Being so restless that it is hard to sit still	0	1	2	3
6. Becoming easily annoyed or irritable	0	1	2	3
7. Feeling afraid as if something awful might happen	0	1	2	3
Add the score for each column				
Total Score (add the column scores) =				

Consider the impact of anxiety on your functioning:
How difficult have these made it for you to do your work, take care of things at home, or getting along with other people?

- ☐ Not difficult at all
- ☐ Somewhat difficult
- ☐ Very difficult
- ☐ Extremely difficult

Source: Spitzer RL, Kroenke K, Williams JBW, Lowe B. A brief measure for assessing generalized anxiety disorder. Arch Inern Med. 2006;166:1092-1097.

03 GAD-7

Generalized Anxiety Disorder Scale

Let's get a starting point as you consider your anxiety and your personal journey to overcoming. Record the total score and date of this 3rd screening. Please read and consider the disclaimers below.

Scoring GAD-7 Anxiety Severity

Total score for the 7 items ranges from 0 to 21.

- ☐ 0–4: minimal anxiety
- ☐ 5–9: mild anxiety
- ☐ 10–14: moderate anxiety
- ☐ 15–21: severe anxiety

Score:_____   Date: _____

Disclaimer: The Generalized Anxiety Disorder 7-item (GAD-7) scale is a self-administered tool designed to screen for and measure the severity of generalized anxiety disorder. While it can provide valuable insights into your anxiety levels, it is not a substitute for professional medical advice, diagnosis, or treatment.
Informational Purposes Only: The results of the GAD-7 are intended for informational and educational purposes only.
Not a Professional Assessment: This tool does not replace a comprehensive evaluation by a licensed mental health professional. Only a qualified healthcare provider can diagnose anxiety or any other mental health disorder.
Seek Professional Help: If you have concerns about your mental health or if the GAD-7 indicates high levels of anxiety, please seek advice from a healthcare provider. If you are experiencing a mental health crisis, contact emergency services immediately.
Limitations: The GAD-7 has limitations and can not capture all aspects of your mental health.

Source: Spitzer RL, Kroenke K, Williams JBW, Lowe B. A brief measure for assessing generalized anxiety disorder. Arch Inern Med. 2006;166:1092-1097.

GAD-7: My Journey

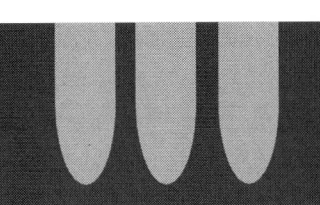

Assessing Overcoming

01 Score on GAD-7 pg. 7

02 Score on GAD-7 pg. 38

03 Score on GAD-7 pg. 54

One of the bravest steps you can take is to decide what healing looks like for you.

OVERCOMING...

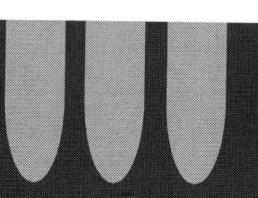

Reflect back on your answers on page 5 when you began the journey through this workbook. What do you want to change, celebrate, or consider? This is YOUR Overcoming Journey!

✦ What is something you have always wanted to do, but haven't yet accomplished?

✦ What barriers are holding you back?

✦ How would your life change if you could take a GIANT leap and JUMP into this?

Your Story...

- Welcome to the journaling section of this workbook. On these blank pages, you will create a masterpiece as unique as YOU!

- Journaling can help you process the difficult emotions and experiences, it can help provide clarity, and it can help you OVERCOME!

- There are many benefits to overcoming anxiety, those include improved physical health, improved relationships, improved sense of self, and improved mental health. READY to begin?

- Be patient and be persistent. Journaling, like most things, can be difficult in the beginning. Be patient with yourself. You will improve over time, with practice. Commit, don't quit! You have much to DISCOVER!

- There are no grades, no right or wrong, there is just your journey to your JUMP!

DAY 1

JOURNALING TO OVERCOME ANXIETY

" Our anxiety does not empty tomorrow of its sorrows, but only empties today of its strengths. "

—— C.H. Spurgeon ——

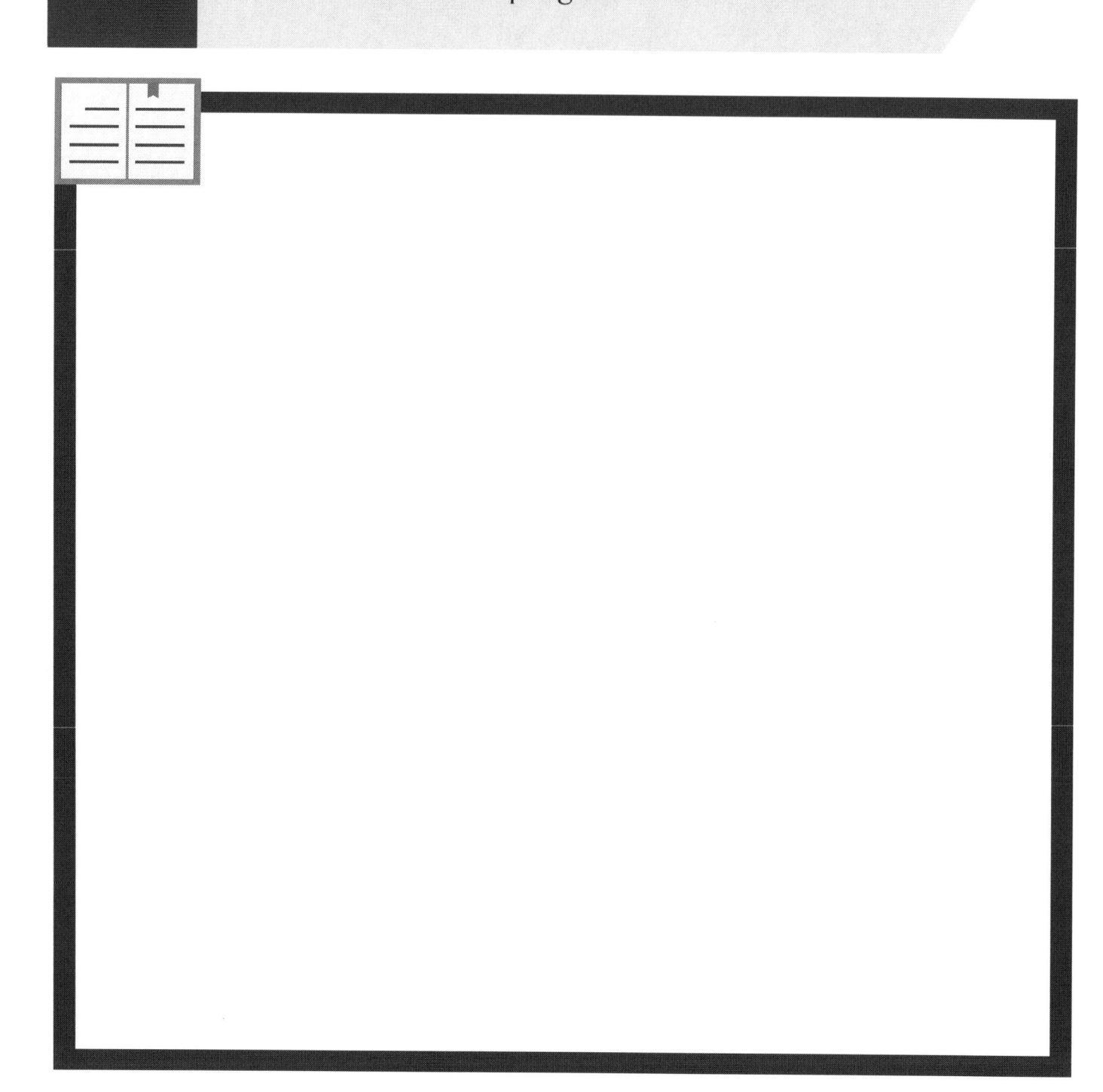

DAY 2

JOURNALING TO OVERCOME ANXIETY

" Anxiety is like a rocking chair. It gives you something to do, but it doesn't get you very far. "

—— Jodi Picoult ——

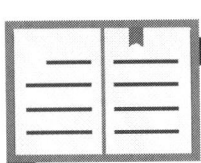

DAY 3

JOURNALING TO OVERCOME ANXIETY

" Worry often gives a small thing a big shadow. "

—Swedish proverb—

DAY 4

JOURNALING TO OVERCOME ANXIETY

"Man is not worried by real problems so much as by his imagined anxieties about real problems."

— Epictetus —

DAY 5

JOURNALING TO OVERCOME ANXIETY

" Worrying is carrying tomorrow's load with today's strength — carrying two days at once. It is moving into tomorrow ahead of time. Worrying doesn't empty tomorrow of its sorrow, it empties today of its strength. "

——————— Corrie ten Boom ———————

DAY 6

JOURNALING TO OVERCOME ANXIETY

"Sometimes the most important thing in a whole day is the rest taken between two deep breaths."

— Etty Hillesum

DAY 7

JOURNALING TO OVERCOME ANXIETY

"Do not anticipate trouble or worry about what may never happen. Keep in the sunlight."

— Benjamin Franklin

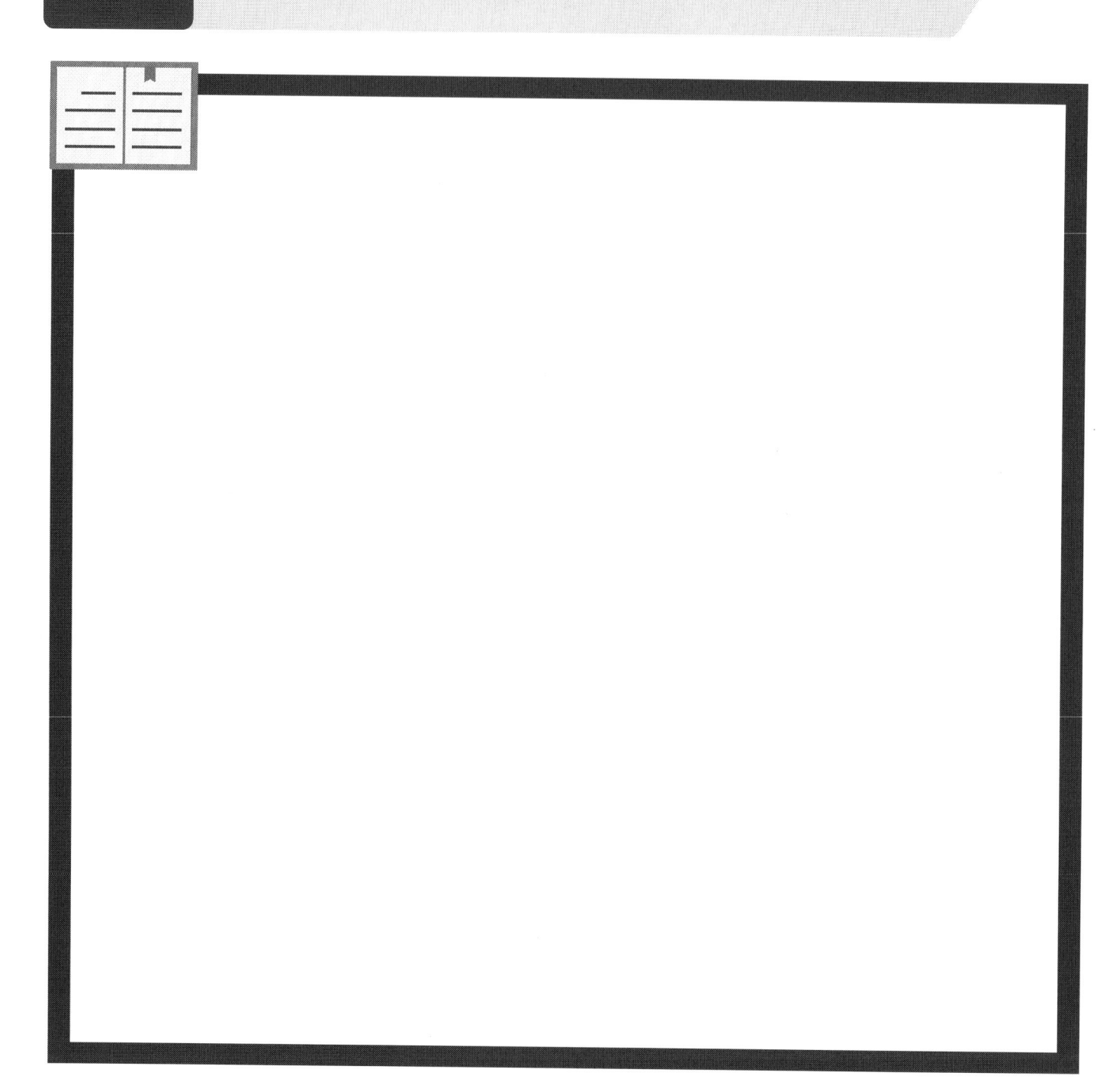

DAY 8

JOURNALING TO OVERCOME ANXIETY

" Don't assume I'm weak because I have panic attacks. You'll never know the amount of strength it takes to face the world every day "

— Unknown —

DAY 9

JOURNALING TO OVERCOME ANXIETY

" Just because I can't explain the feelings causing my anxiety doesn't make them less valid "

—— Lauren Elizabeth ——

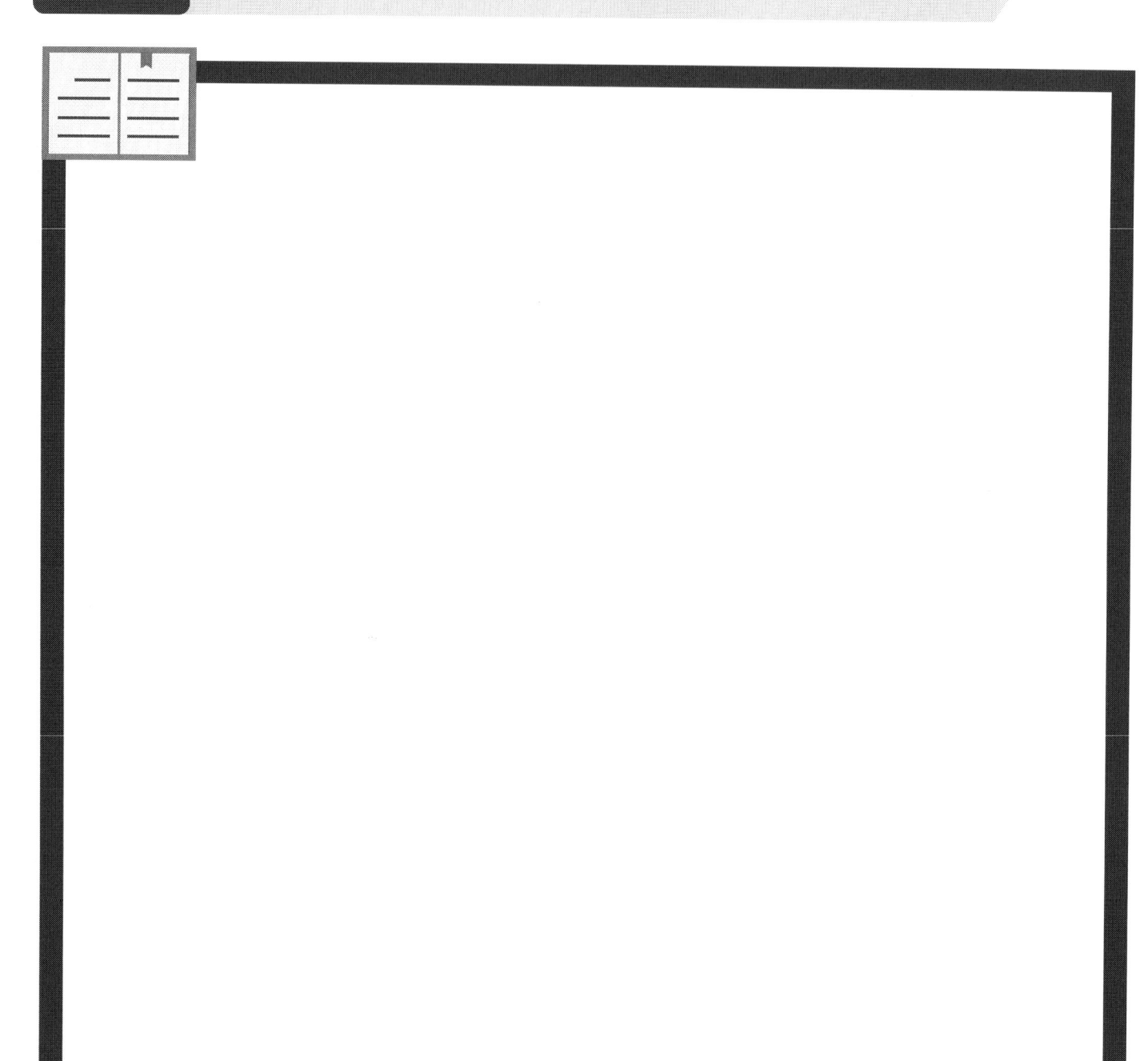

DAY 10

JOURNALING TO OVERCOME ANXIETY

" Every time you are tempted to react in the same old way, ask if you want to be a prisoner of the past or a pioneer of the future. "

—— Deepak Chopra ——

DAY 11

JOURNALING TO OVERCOME ANXIETY

"He who fears he shall suffer, already suffers what he fears."

— Michel de Montaigne

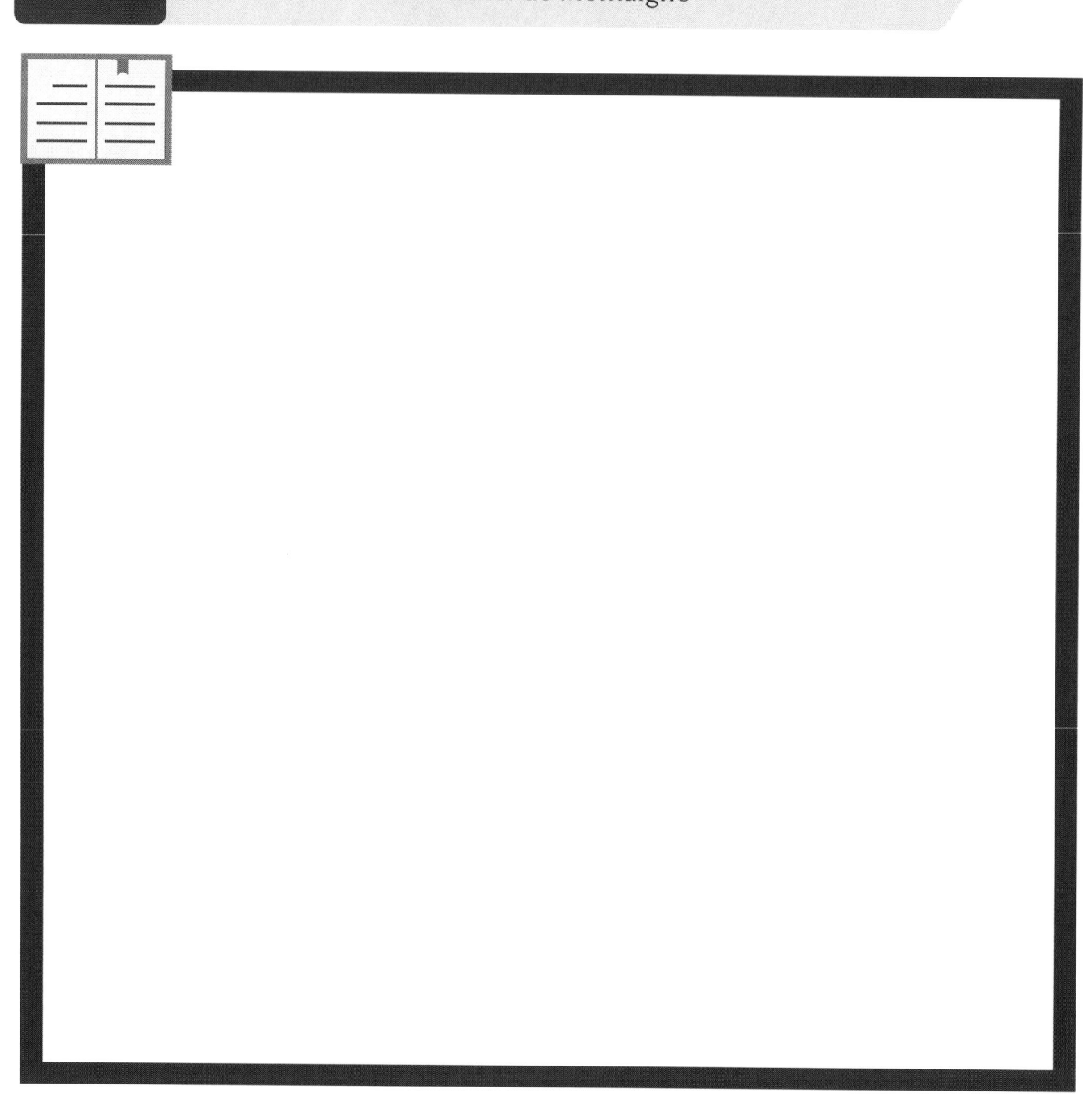

DAY 12

JOURNALING TO OVERCOME ANXIETY

"If you want to conquer the anxiety of life, live in the moment, live in the breath."

— Amit Ray

DAY 13

JOURNALING TO OVERCOME ANXIETY

"If you always do what you've always done, you'll always get what you've always got."

— Stephen Hayes

DAY 14

JOURNALING TO OVERCOME ANXIETY

" Nothing diminishes anxiety faster than action. "

—— Walter Anderson ——

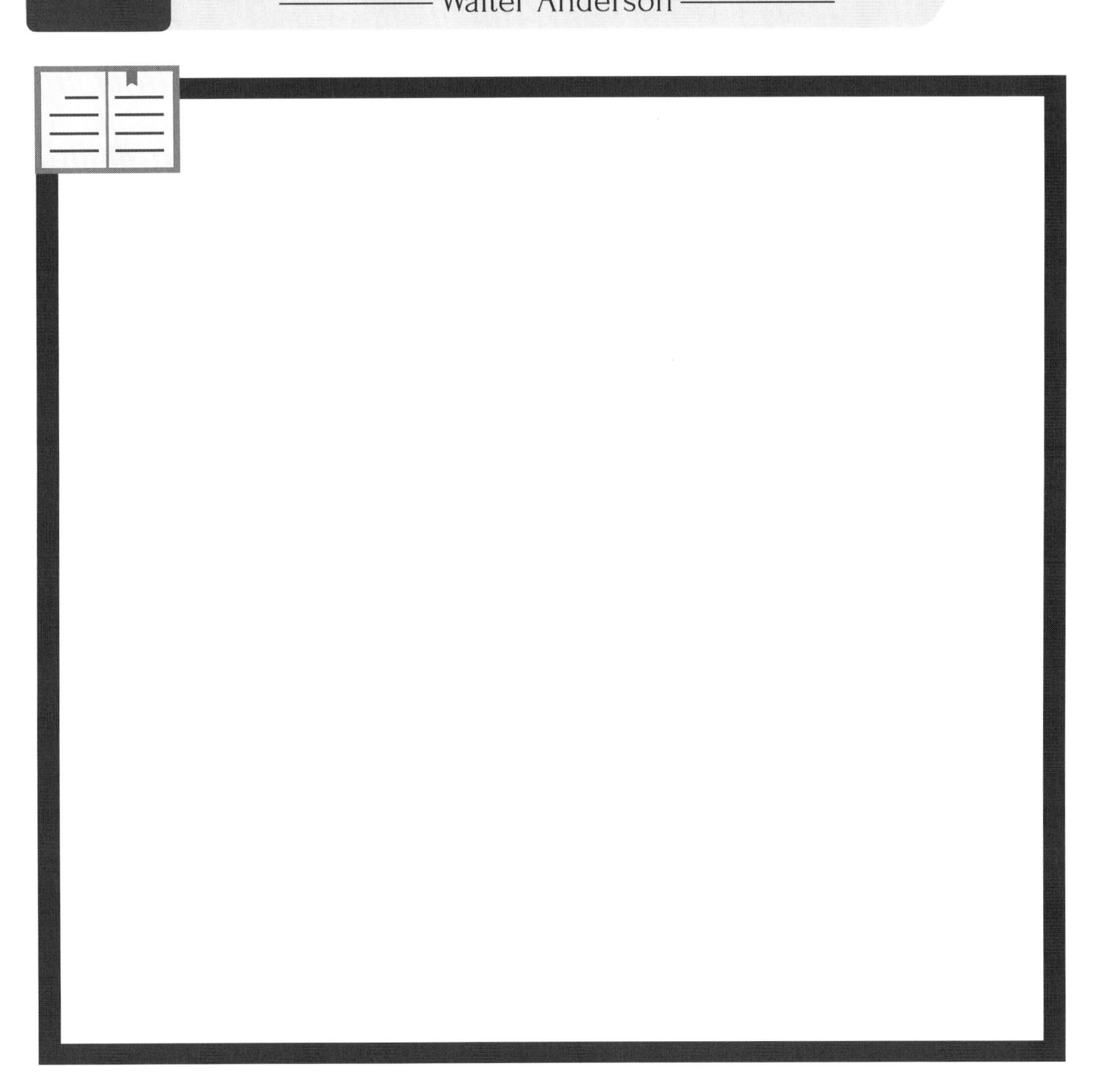

DAY 15

JOURNALING TO OVERCOME ANXIETY

"You may not control all the events that happen to you, but you can decide not to be reduced by them."

— Maya Angelou

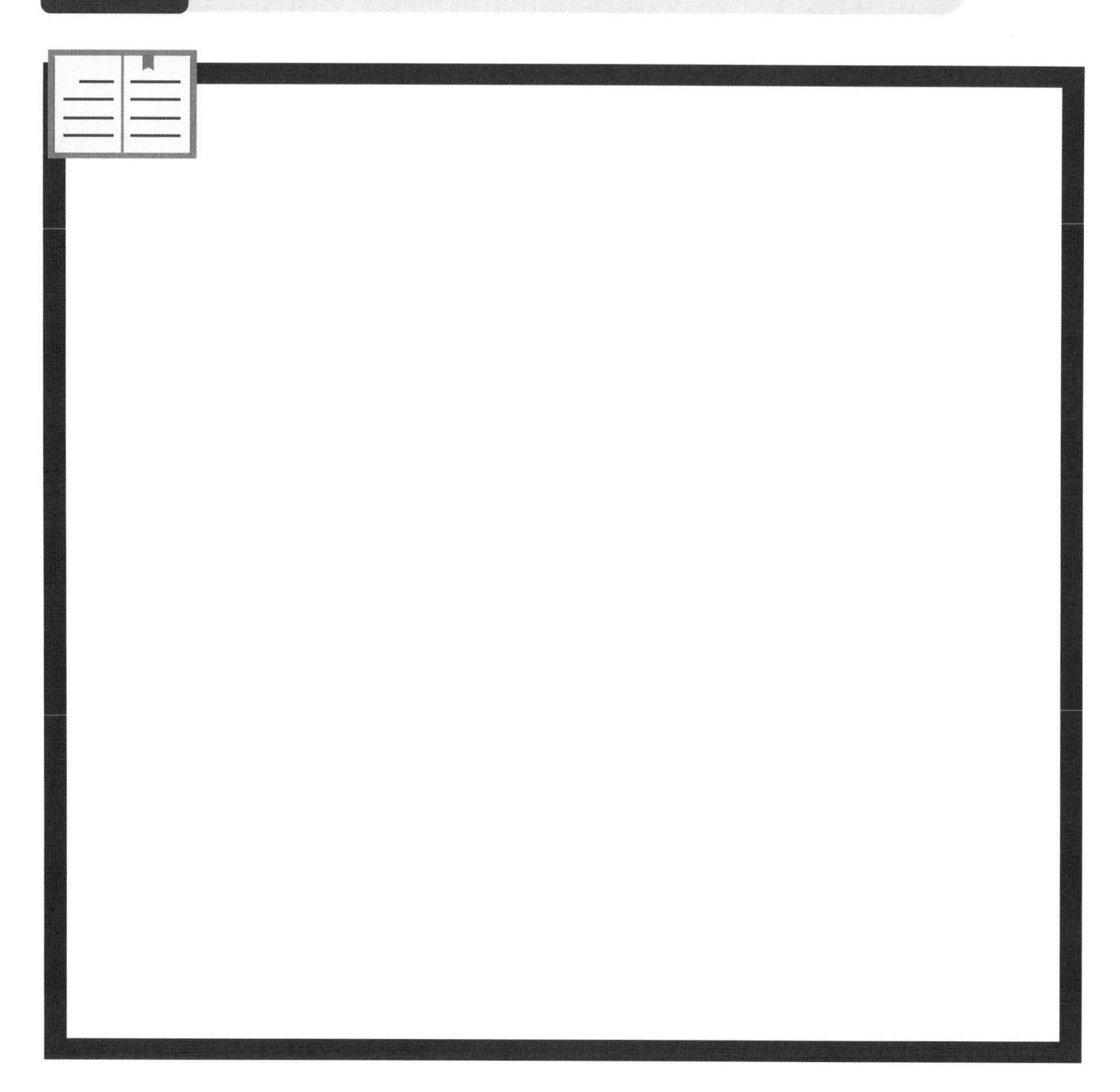

DAY 16

JOURNALING TO OVERCOME ANXIETY

"Instead of worrying about what you cannot control, shift your energy to what you can create."

— Roy Bennett

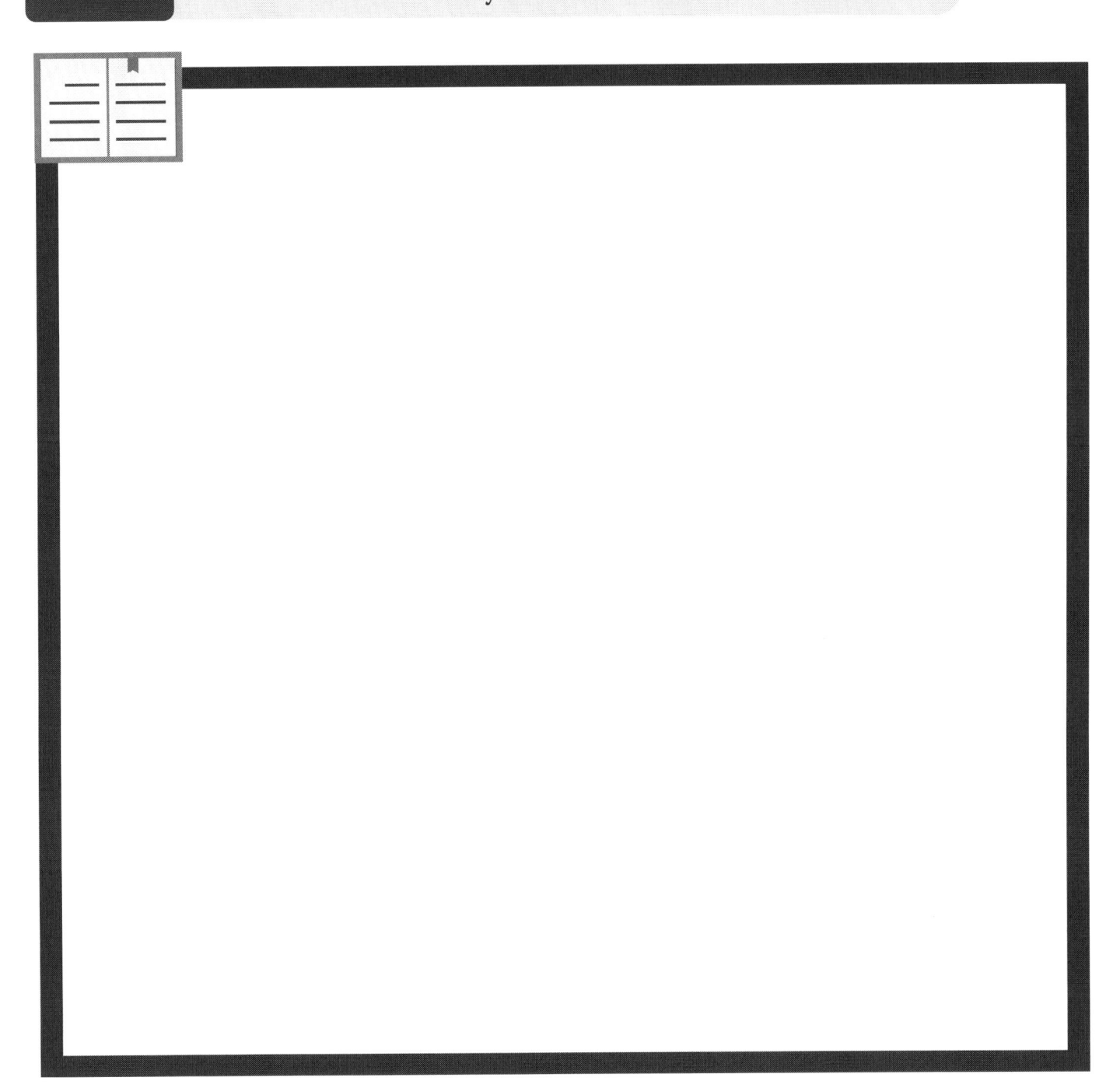

DAY 17

JOURNALING TO OVERCOME ANXIETY

" *Good humor is a tonic for mind and body. It is the best antidote for anxiety and depression... It lightens human burdens. It is the direct route to serenity and contentment.* "

— Grenville Kleiser —

DAY 18

JOURNALING TO OVERCOME ANXIETY

"What lies behind us and what lies before us are tiny matters compared to what lies within us."

—Henry S. Haskins

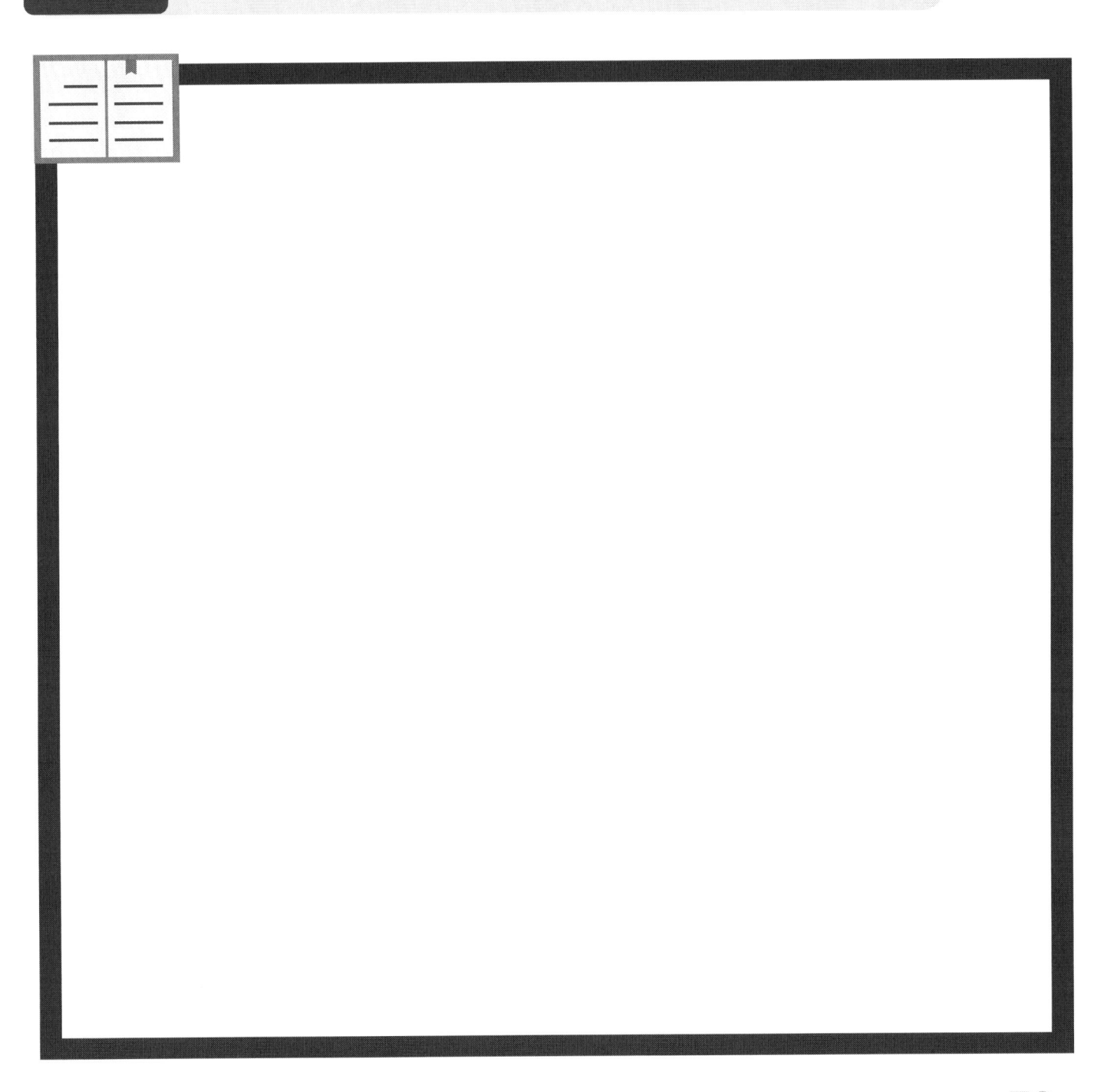

DAY 19

JOURNALING TO OVERCOME ANXIETY

" Difficult roads often lead to beautiful destinations. The best is yet to come. "

— Zig Ziglar

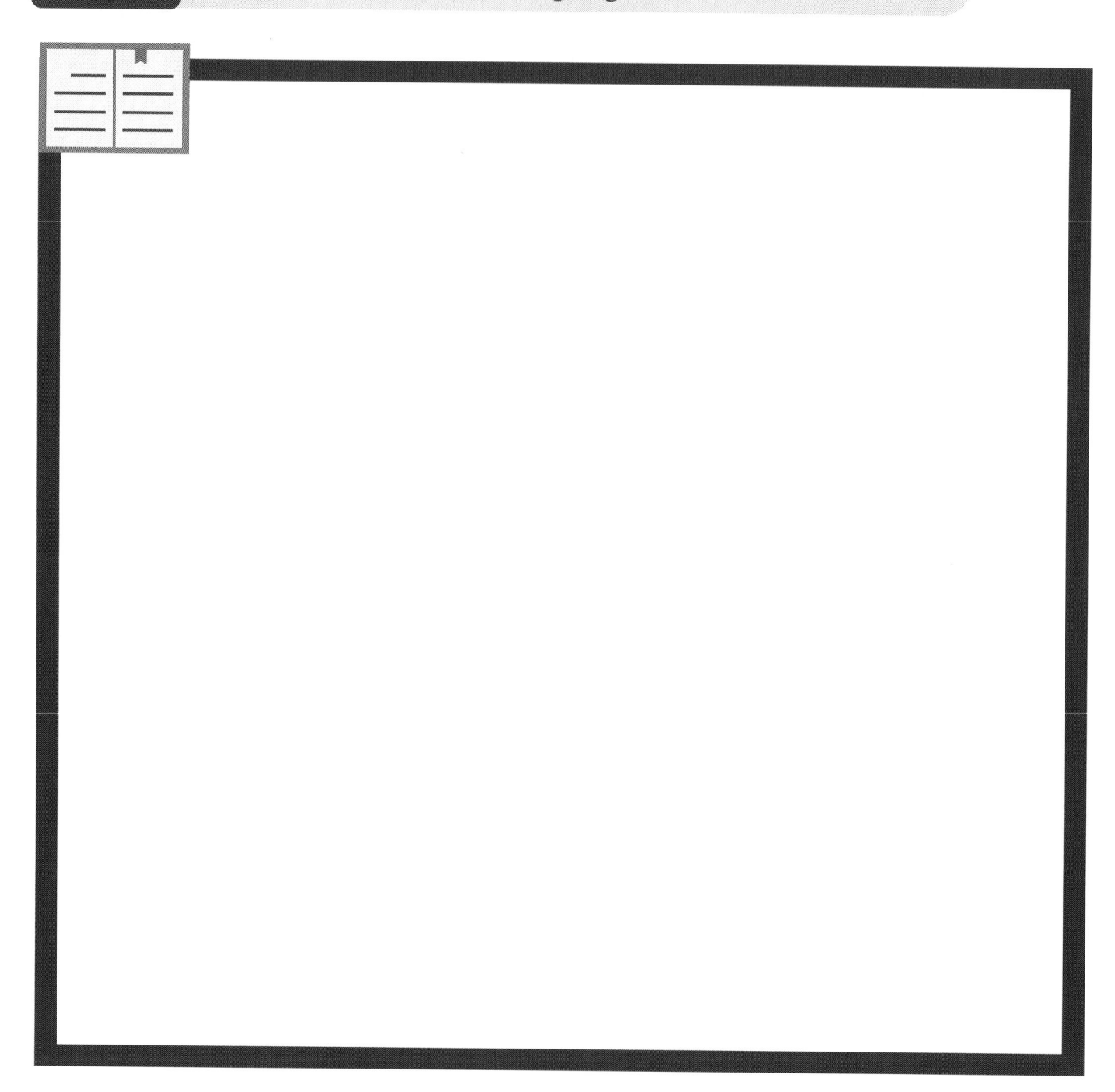

DAY 20

JOURNALING TO OVERCOME ANXIETY

" Be not afraid of life. Believe that life is worth living, and your belief will help create the fact. "

—— William James ——

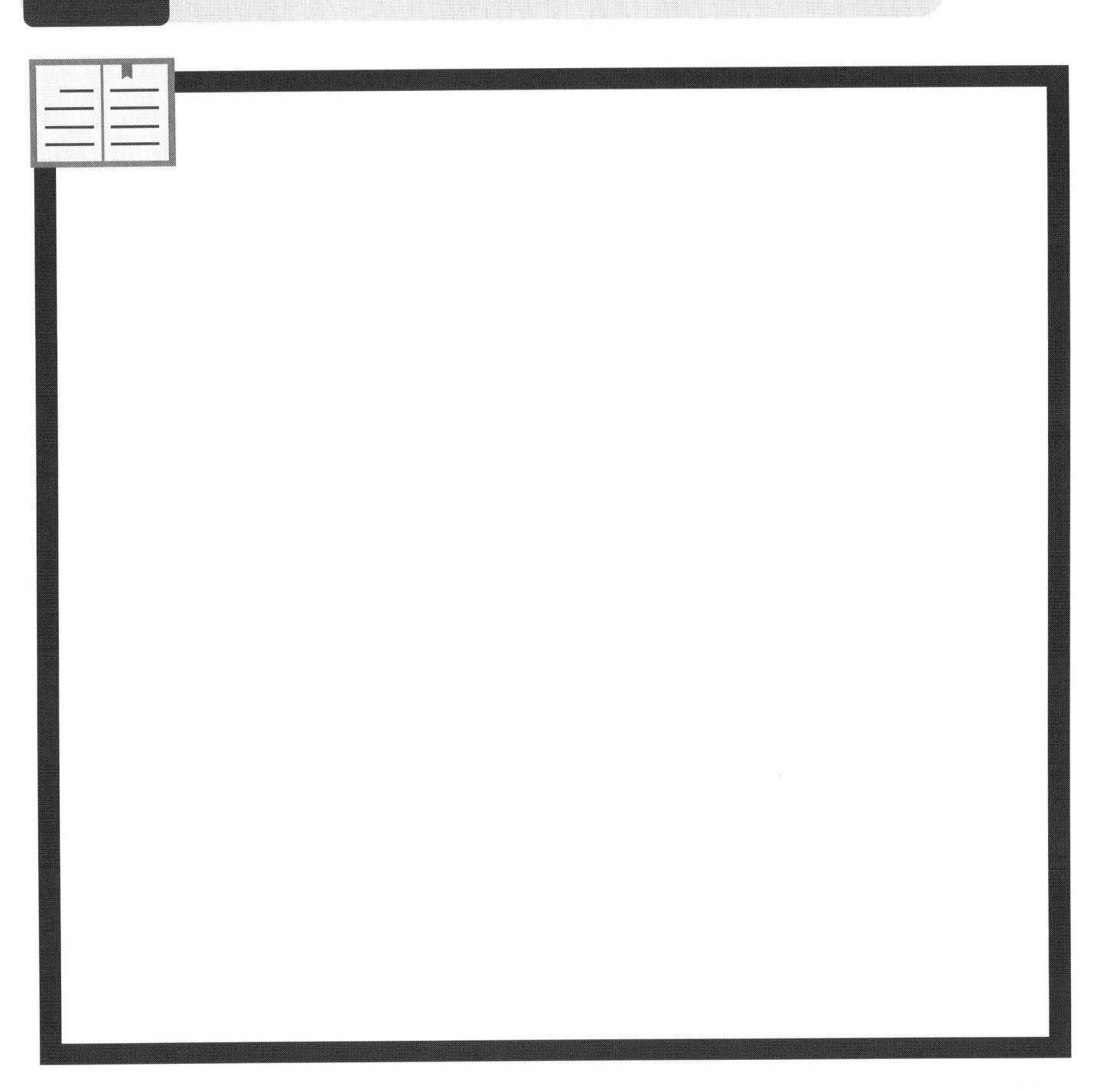

DAY 21

JOURNALING TO OVERCOME ANXIETY

"Almost everything will work again if you unplug it for a few minutes, including you."

——— Anne Lamott ———

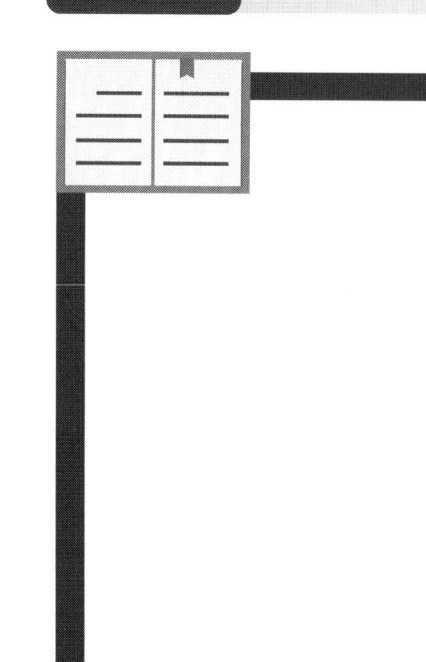

DAY 22

" JOURNALING TO OVERCOME ANXIETY

Some days, doing 'the best we can' may still fall short of what we would like to be able to do, but life isn't perfect — on any front — and doing what we can with what we have is the most we should expect of ourselves or anyone else. "

— Mister Rogers —

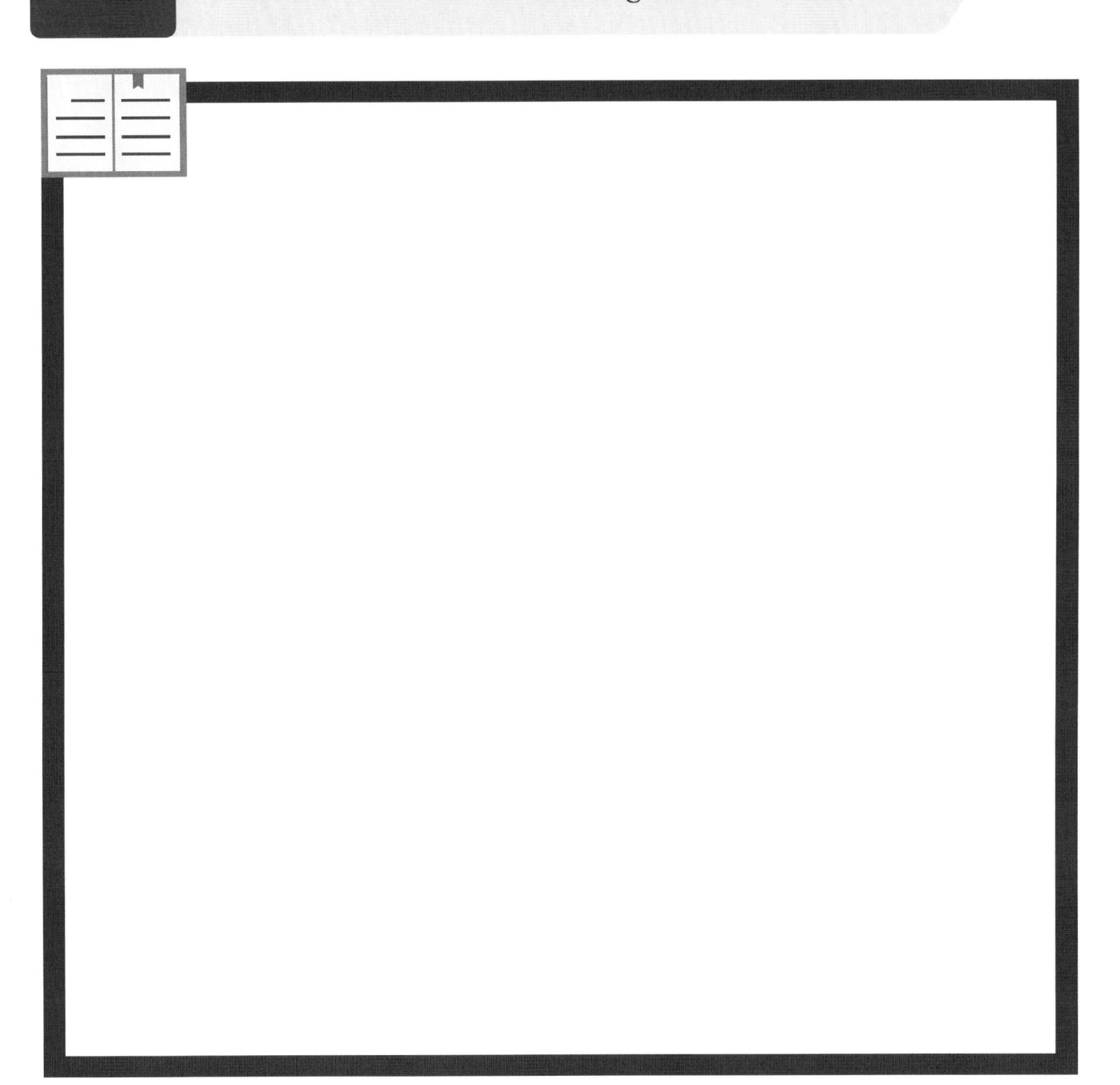

DAY 23

JOURNALING TO OVERCOME ANXIETY

"Surrender to what is, let go of what was, and have faith in what will be."

— Sonia Ricotti

DAY 24

JOURNALING TO OVERCOME ANXIETY

"Grant me the serenity to accept the things I cannot change, the courage to change the things I can, and the wisdom to know the difference."

—— Reinhold Niebuhr ——

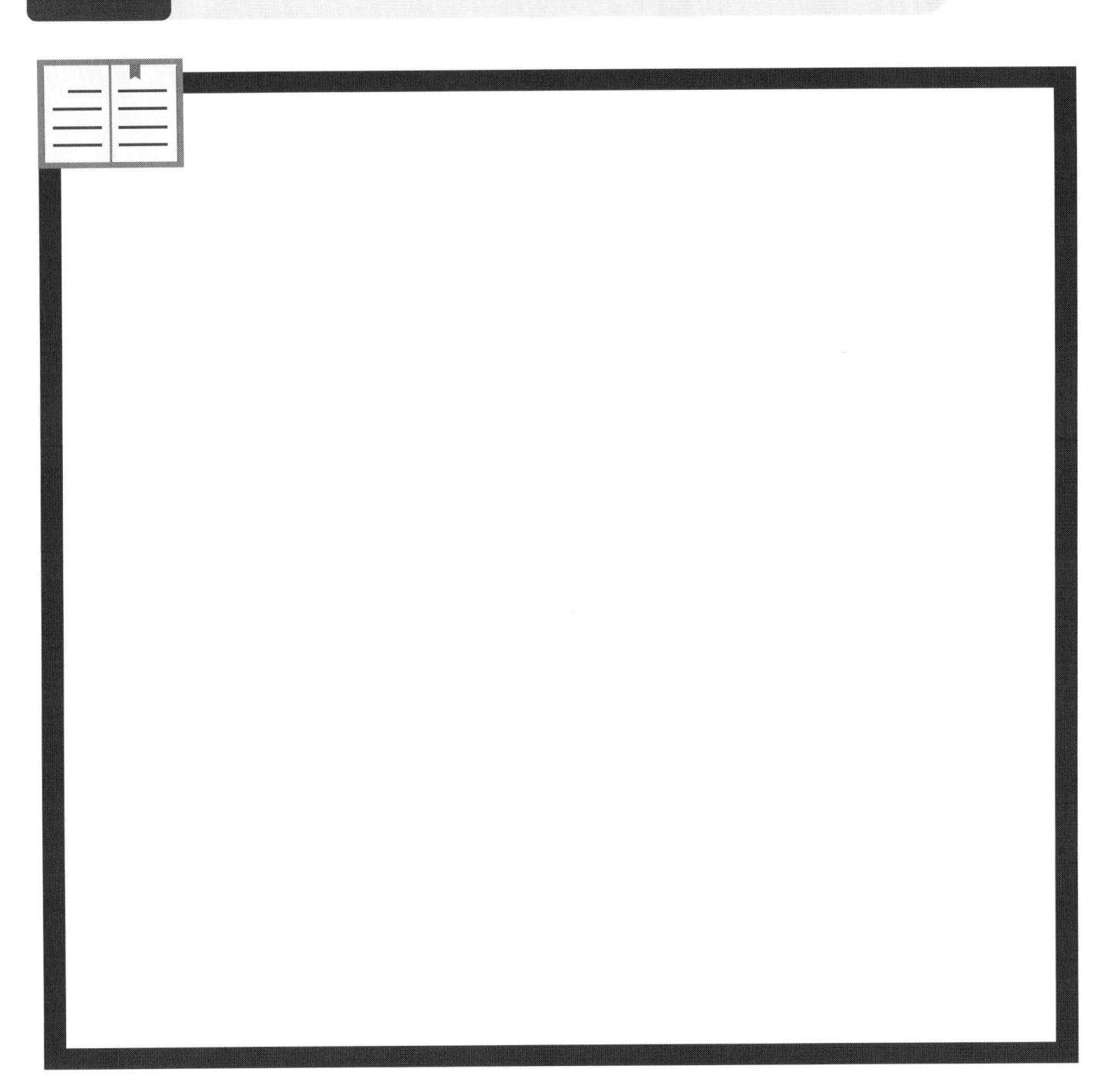

DAY 25

JOURNALING TO OVERCOME ANXIETY

"In the end, it is important to remember that we cannot become what we need to be by remaining where we are."

— Max De Pree

DAY 26

JOURNALING TO OVERCOME ANXIETY

" I've had a lot of worries in my life, most of which never happened. "

— Mark Twain —

DAY 27

JOURNALING TO OVERCOME ANXIETY

" *Life is like riding a bicycle. To keep your balance, you must keep moving* "

—— Albert Einstein ——

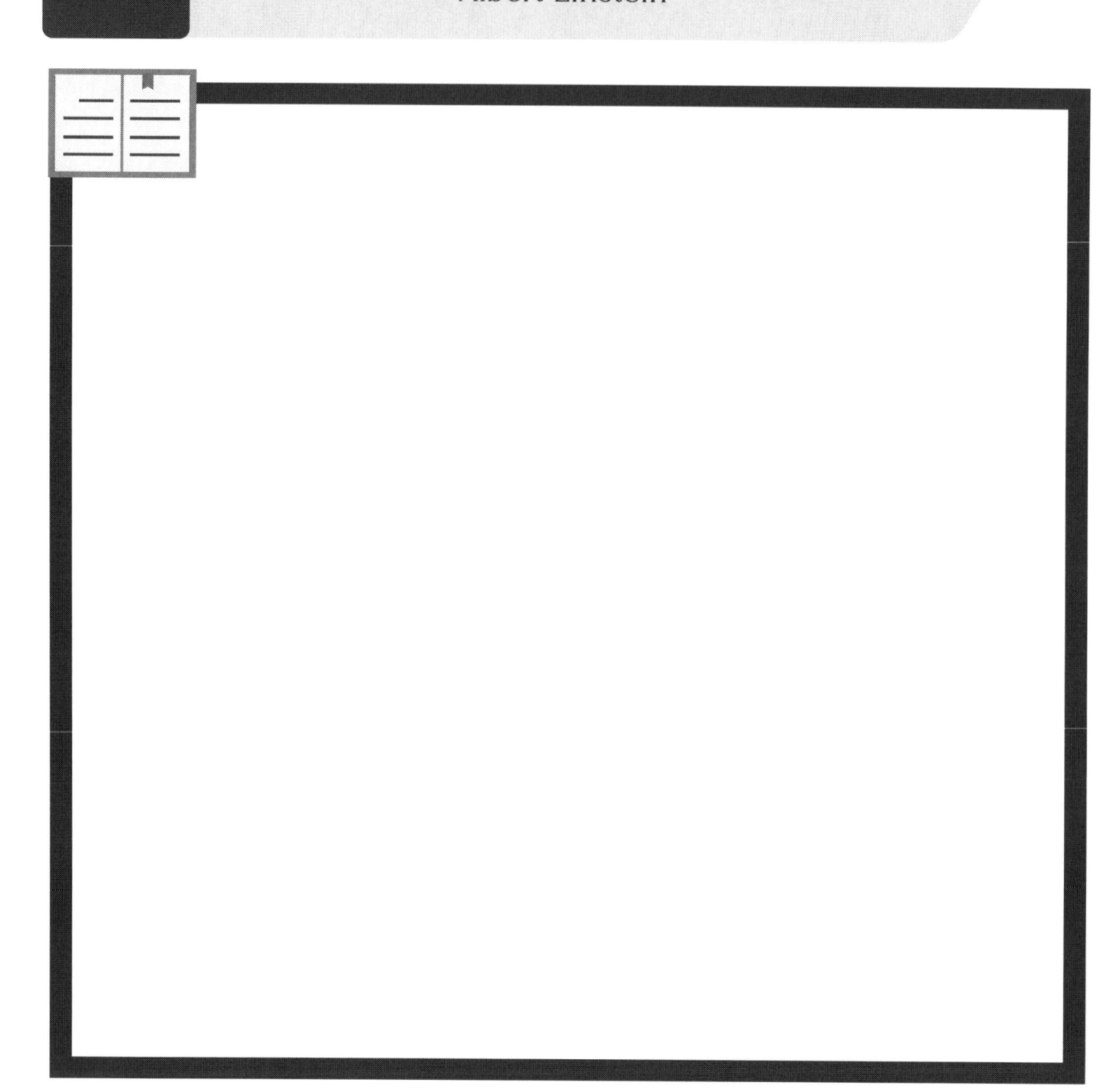

DAY 28

JOURNALING TO OVERCOME ANXIETY

" Who of you by worrying can add a single hour to his life?

———— Jesus ————

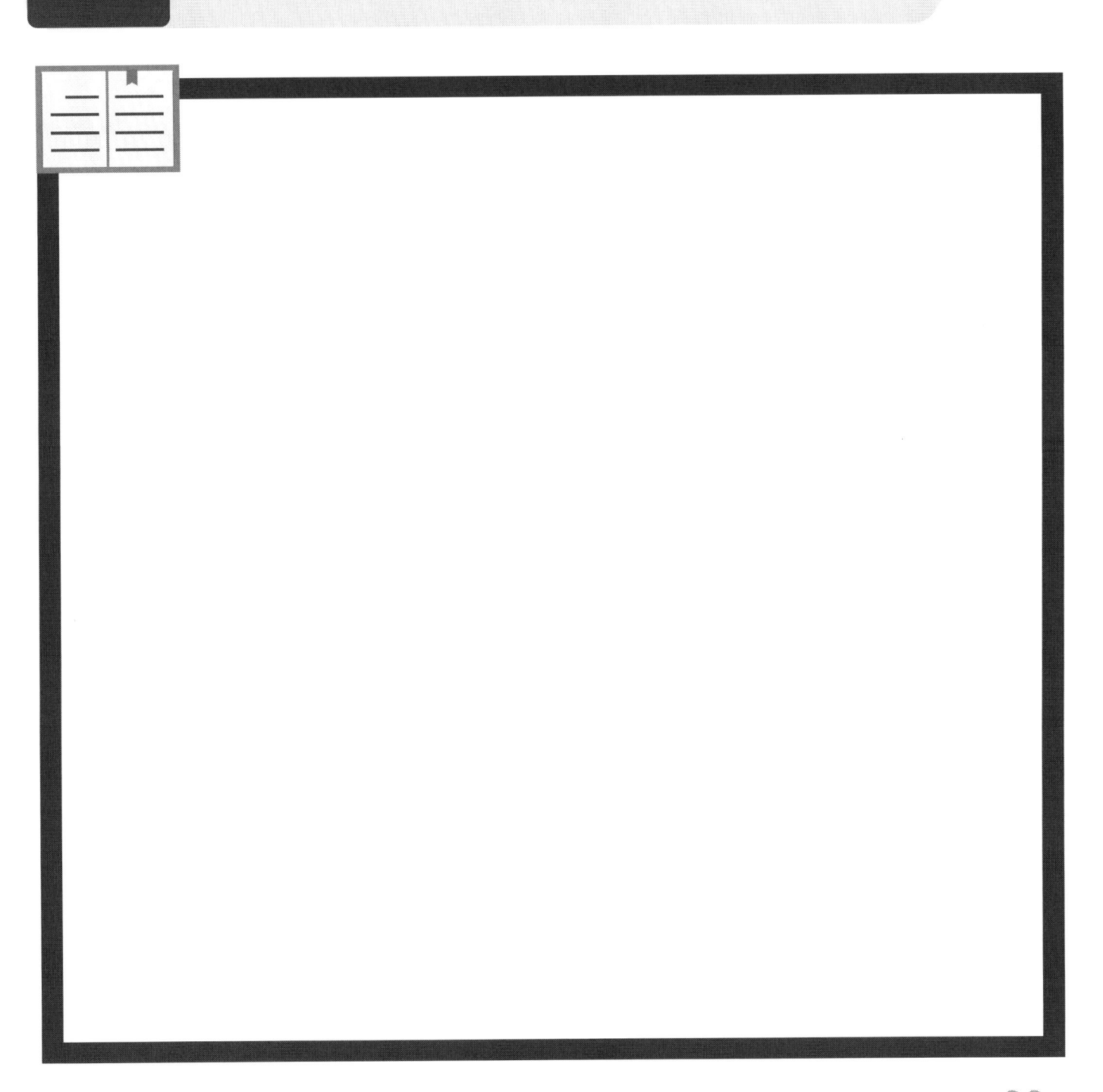

DAY 29

JOURNALING TO OVERCOME ANXIETY

"The only thing we have to fear is fear itself."

— Franklin Delano Roosevelt

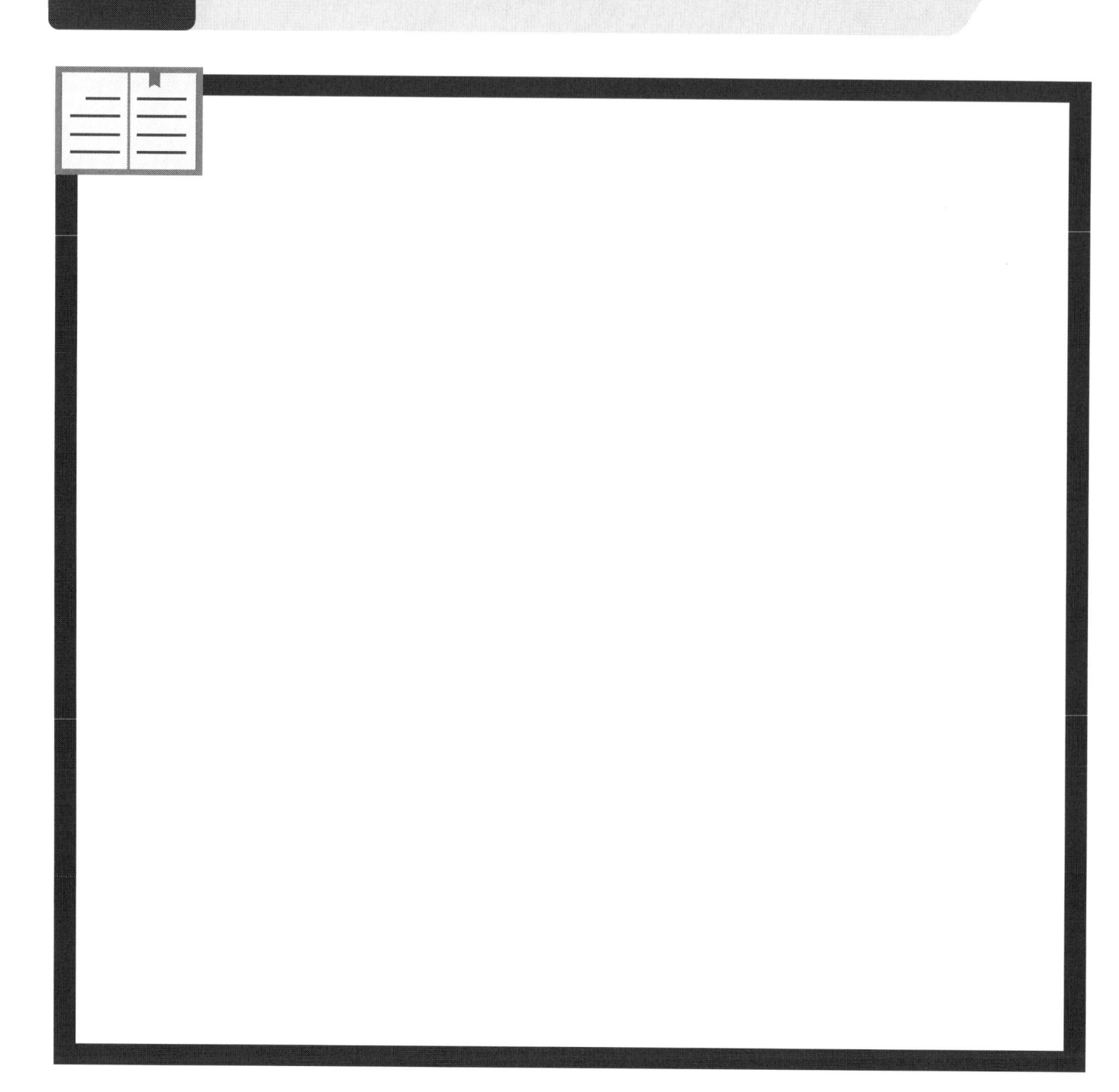

DAY 30

JOURNALING TO OVERCOME ANXIETY

"If you can't fly then run, if you can't run then walk, if you can't walk then crawl, but whatever you do you have to keep moving forward."

— Martin Luther King Jr

DAY 31

JOURNALING TO OVERCOME ANXIETY

" Just keep swimming. "

——— Dory ———

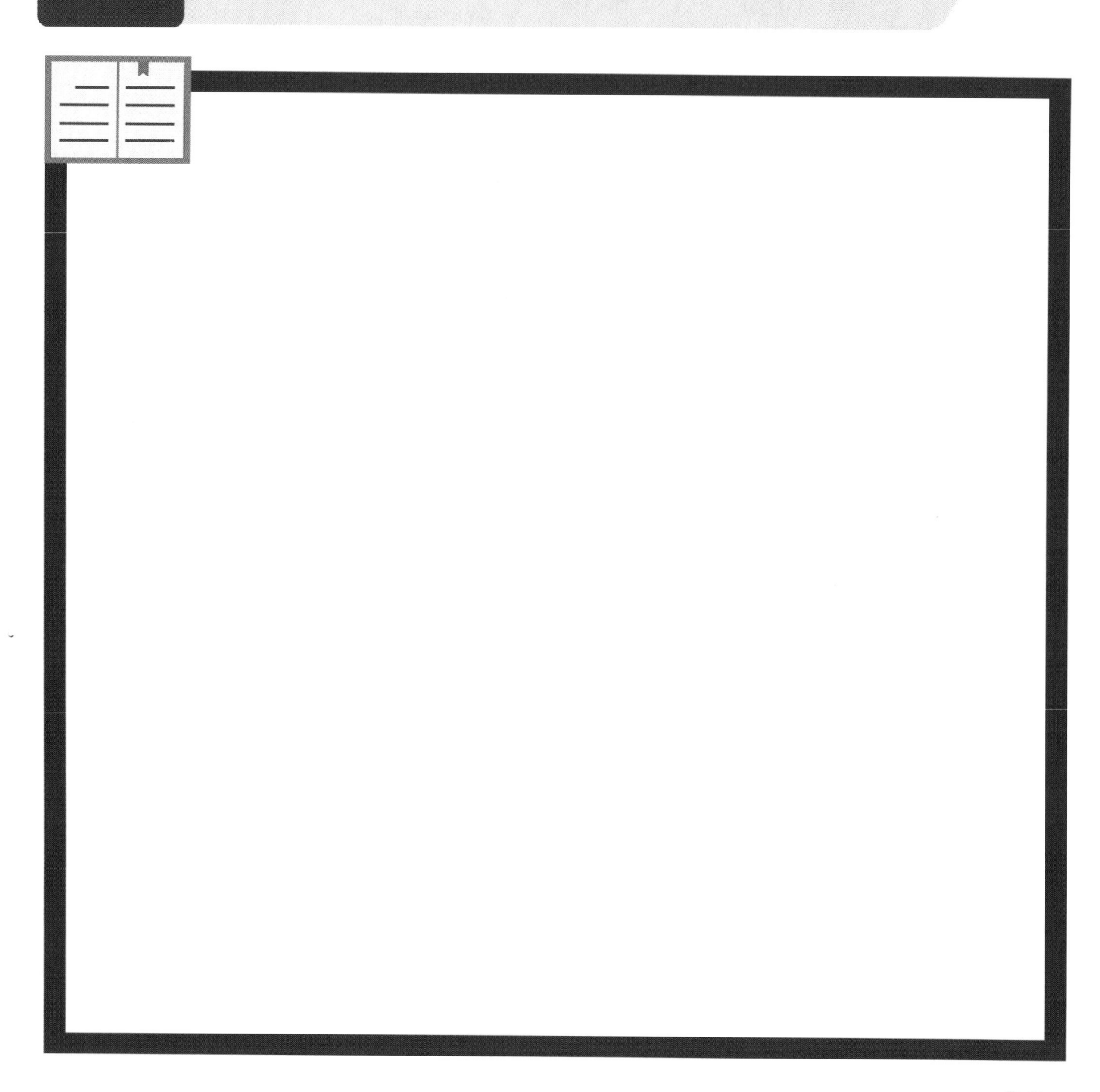

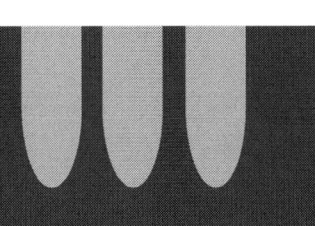

You did it!

- You did it! You completed your anxiety workbook. How do you feel? Can you pause, reflect, and choose to celebrate your journey?

- You are not alone! Help is available. I love to say, "The healthiest people on the planet spend time on our sofas!" If there is more work to do, consider this a great start, and keep at it!

- What are you most proud of? What do you want to share with others? What are you realizing still needs to be done?

- What have you overcome? What has happened to you? How have you survived? I am proud that you made it here, and I can't wait to see what you do next!

- Stay tuned to www.theovercomingseries.com for MORE books in this series, freebies, videos, and more! I would love to see a review on Amazon and hear from you! Follow me on social media @theovercomingseries

Made in the USA
Columbia, SC
10 August 2024